I've ... y ... Lucky Number

I've Got your Lucky Number

Understand its vibration and impact on your personality and relationships

S. J. Culbert, The Fortune Teller

W. Foulsham & Co. Ltd.

London • New York • Toronto • Cape Town • Sydney

To my Mother,
who certaintly got her numbers right.

W. Foulsham & Company Limited
Yeovil Road, Slough, Berkshire, SL1 4JH

ISBN 0-572-01398-1

Copyright © 1986 W. Foulsham & Co. Ltd.

All rights reserved.
The Copyright Act (1956) prohibits (subject to certain
very limited exceptions) the making of copies of any
copyright work or of a substantial part of such a work,
including the making of copies by photocopying or
similar process. Written permission to make a copy
or copies must therefore normally be obtained from the
publisher in advance. It is advisable also to consult
the publisher if in any doubt as to the legality of any
copying which is to be undertaken.

Printed in Great Britain and St. Edmundsbury Press,
Bury St. Edmunds.

CONTENTS

INTRODUCTION

Ask any man, woman or child in the street if they know what astrology is and they will be able to give you an adequate answer. Ask that same person if they have ever heard of numerology and it would be like asking a child of ten to solve a problem in pure mathematics. Numerology, more fancifully known as metaphysical mathematics, is for some unknown reason little known, publicised or understood. Why is this so?

The ancient art of astrology, with which we are so familiar, is based upon a planetary placement at the time of birth which predetermines our abilities and personalities, and yet each planet has its number value from the Sun.

Palmistry is a map of those same planetary forces in our hands, and yet is seldom related to numerology even though we have eight fingers and two thumbs. Tarot cards, though in different suites, are also numbered and laid out in numerical order for consultation. And yet we, for some unknown reason, fail to use the system which rules all forms of communication, that of numerology.

Pythagoras, Socrates and Cheiro all understood and recognised the significance of numbers in our lives. I have set out in this manual to familiarise this ancient system. Unlike my fellow authors on the subject, I base my interpretation of the numbers solely on the birth vibration, paying little attention to the name number. This is based on the understanding that your astrological chart or palm print fails to change on the whim of a change of name. Name numbers affect more our environment than our true selves. The birth number is our foundation. I have therefore endeavoured to lay before you that basic foundation from which we all build our futures – for good or bad.

THE ROOTS OF NUMEROLOGY

Numerology has its roots in the ancient Babylonian and Caladian cultures. Whoever first sat down and devised the oracular form that we see in general use today has yet to be identified. Several systems have evolved over the course of the centuries and, however strange the ideas behind each system, one thing is they all, however complex, manage to arrive at the same answer.

Numerology has not always been as popular in Britain as it is today. In fact, it was relatively unheard of, except by serious students of the occult, until the Victorian era of Cheiro. Though Cheiro's system differs in the values that he gave to individual letters and sounds from that of the more popularised systems in use today, I feel certain that he much popularised numerology here.

From the time of Cheiro onwards, the numbers of students of numerology grew. With the increase in students there was an increase in published matter on the subject, informing the greater masses. And so today, with our freedom to read and speak in an enlightened, unpersecuted society, that which had been darkened for so long has been brought into the light.

HOW TO FIND YOUR BIRTH NUMBER

The calculation to find your own personal birth number is simplicity itself. You simply break the birth date down into three parts, add them together and reduce them to a single digit by further addition. Example: The twenty-seventh October 1967 would become $27 + 10 = 37$ plus the total of the year of birth, in this case $1 + 9 + 6 + 7 = 23$. Now simply add the total of the day and month to the total of the year, in this case $37 + 23 = 60$. Then simply add the total to itself, in this case $6 + 0 = 6$. Therefore if you were born on 27.10.67, your birth number is 60/6.

In this system totals are added to totals. If you wish to find if there are lesser forces at work for you, it is possible for those with double-digit days and months to reduce them, i.e. 27 becomes 9, 10th month becomes 1. In the case of 27th October 1967, the final sum would be $9 + 1 + 23 = 33/6$. It must be remembered, however, that this is a lesser force and cannot compete with the full birth number.

These birth numbers have been widely researched by myself as a practising clairvoyant for many years. While it is not possible to take into account the individual hereditary background and environment of individuals, it is possible to determine the personal vibration.

Remember, the law lord may protect the society we all live in through his adjudication in court, while poor old Joe Bloggs may simply be a law-abiding citizen. Yet both are known in their own environments for their steadfast honesty. So when you read these pages you must endeavour to try to relate them to the realities of your lifestyle.

This manuscript is available as a computer manual to run on a Tandy radioshack model 3/4. A card version is also in being, relating the birth numbers to an astrological spread of twelve houses. Each card has 24 meanings, one for upright and one for reversed in each house position. It should then be a simple matter to relate the force of the card to the subject matter of the astrological house it occupies, bringing a new form of tarot card without complications. Just what the new age of Aquarius demands.

After each of the birth number evaluations, you will find a useful table for you to fill in with your own observations of family, friends and colleagues. Use these to help you learn more about the people around you, and to help them learn more about themselves. You can also use the tables to compare the positive and negative characteristics of your friends with those of their partner.

Once you have discovered your birth number, you can also find out the characteristics of your alter ego. Subtract your birth number from 70 to discover the opposite character which would complete you. For example, if your birth number is 20, subtract this from 70, giving an opposite birth number of 50.

BIRTH NUMBERS

The whole of the birth number reduced to a single digit is the sum total of the personality. The preceding two numbers are the facets of the personality.

Your birth number is
13/4

Your lucky numbers are: 4, 13, 22, 31, 40, 49, 58, 67, 76, 85.
Your lucky colours are: blue, green and indigo.
Your best partners are: other 4s, 1s and 8.

Your character
As a positive ruling 4, you are a builder, both on the material and
the intellectual planes, always busy, mentally and physically. A 4
makes a splendid bookmaker or mechanic; he is mathematical,
methodical, a master of detail and routine. He is a splendid
builder of systems for greater economy. His ambitions are of a
personal nature for his own self-development.

All 4s need a firm platform from which to operate. Once this is
achieved, they find themselves free from the fears and worries
that held them back from their ideals and dreams in the first place.
Go on, commit yourself.

As a negative 4 you are despondent, buried beneath adverse
circumstances, financial limitations and hard work, a plodder
without any desire for intellectual development.

Your numbers vibrate to the planets Sun, Jupiter and Uranus.

A 13/4 is a fair old mixture; the combinations would give the
casual observer the idea that you are a little too self-centred, as
your carefree attitude can be externally self-orientated. This, however, is not the case. It is, in fact, a cover in order that you may mix
in the hustle and bustle of everyday life with at least an appearance of security. You are in fact very sensitive to the words and
actions of others but feel that it is weak to show too much of your

real self in case others take advantage. You are, in fact, willing to help those who help themselves.

The 13/4s find it necessary to dominate their own lifestyle in order that they can keep their inner fears and worries under control. They seek stability and yet never appear to be content with what they have actually achieved. They should learn to take one step at a time, as they are likely to spread themselves too thin on the ground and dissipate their energies. A firm commitment in land or property should give them the basis of a secure lifestyle.

The negative 13/4s become too dominant in their own and their close family's lives. They can come to believe that all will go wrong unless they have the control. They can shy away from commitments, fearing the consequences.

Your birth number is 13/4

Name: Date of birth:

Lucky number: Lucky colour:

Partner's birth number:

Positive characteristics:

Negative characteristics:

Your birth number is
14/5

Your lucky numbers are: 5, 14, 23, 32, 41, 50, 59, 68, 77, 86, 95.
Your lucky colours are: scarlet, orange and wine.
Your best partners are: other 5s, 2s or 7s.

Your character
As a ruling 5 person you are a wanderer. Mental activity is strong with these people; they don't just seem to be able to find the neutral gear as far as mental activity is concerned, always full of bright ideas and projects. The number is sometimes called the freedom seeker, as the ruling 5 is always on the go, loves to travel and hates restrictions of any kind. Fives are best employed in a job that has few restrictions as they hate regulations. Quick-witted and with few inhibitions, these people are usually found in the positions of stress that others find difficult to control.

The negative 5, on the other hand, is the chatterbox who rants on endlessly and says very little, too preoccupied with his own ego and self-praise to notice that he is boring the pants off his friends. Ulcers or stress-oriented illnesses prevail and there can be a tendency to mental burn-outs which leave him dazed and disorientated.

Your numbers vibrate to the planets Sun and Uranus.

As a 14/5 you are quick-witted, versatile, original and inventive. Freedom of self-expression and action are very important to you, although insufficient rest could lead to nervous tension, so beware.

This combination of birth numbers indicates a life of variety and change. Progressive and original people with this birth number are constantly investigating life and seeking new experiences. You are more likely to have broken away from family ties earlier in life in order that you could venture out into the unknown to test your independence. You would rather be non-committal in relationships as you fear restrictions. With the ability to communicate new ideas and concepts to others, you should have no problem in selling yourself in romance or business. You should, however, remember that you only have one pair of hands to work with.

As a negative 14/5 you fear the changes that you wish would happen, ever hoping that someone else will shelter you from the uncertainties ahead. You become nervous, scared and frightened of the unknown, wishing it would go away.

You need to develop your extrovert side instead of reserving it for safe, secure situations with people you know. Commit yourself to a project that you feared and, with the experience it gives you, start life anew.

Work in sales, travel or metaphysics would suit a 14/5. They love to excel, but hate to be tied down to a routine.

Your birth number is 14/5

Name: Date of birth:

Lucky number: Lucky colour:

Partner's birth number:

Positive characteristics:

Negative characteristics:

Your birth number is
15/6

Your lucky numbers are: 6, 15, 24, 33, 42, 51, 60, 69, 87, 78, 96.
Your lucky colours are: bitter chocolate, green and deep sea blue.
Your best partners are: other 6s, 9s and 3s.

Your character
As a ruling 6 person you are kind and gentle-hearted, generous and peaceful, striving constantly to put right other people's wrongs. You are known for your adoration of children and the beautiful, artistic things in life with which you try to surround yourself. You would make an excellent nurse or social worker and can see both sides of most coins.

You do like an active social life though you need the knowledge that you have a safe, secure home to retreat to. You may be very house-proud as you like your surroundings to look pleasing and be admired by visitors.

You can, on the negative side, be very vain, always admiring your own accomplishments and expecting others to do the same. Your ardent love for the home and family can cause you to find it difficult to break away on your own.

Your numbers vibrate to the planets Sun, Mercury and Venus.

As a 15/6 you are cheerful, optimistic and friendly with a magnetic personality. You get on very well with the young, no matter how old you are yourself. You are emotionally forceful and idealistic, with artistic or musical ability. Strong will power for good or bad, coupled with the drive to succeed whatever the cost, could see you get to the top of your chosen career. You will, however, seek the approval of those you love in new enterprises.

You know how to turn on the charm in order to achieve what you desire. You will like your home to be a safe retreat from the hustle and bustle of everyday life and would prefer mental rather than physical labour. In partnerships, marital or business, you would need to earn your own money and have a degree of independence if it were to succeed. You need to feel wanted, but only when you're in the right mood.

As a negative 15/6 you misuse your charm to get your own way and satisfy your insecurities. This, in turn, leaves you with no respect for your chosen partner which, in the end, can only lead to separation.

You need to learn to ask others to do only that which you would be prepared to do yourself in similar circumstances. If you learn to live by this rule, you will not only earn the respect of your peers, but their admiration.

Your birth number is $^{15}/_{6}$

Name: Date of birth:

Lucky number: Lucky colour:

Partner's birth number:

Positive characteristics:

Negative characteristics:

Your lucky numbers are: 7, 16, 25, 34, 43, 52, 61, 70, 89, 98.
Your lucky colours are: sky blue, silver and sea green.
Your best partners are: other 7s, 5s or 2s.

Your character
As a ruling 7 person you are highly intuitive, constantly gathering information on the mysteries of life but seldom talking about them. A deep thinker but not a great doer, you are seldom understood by others and tend to withdraw. Your inability to express the real you can often lead you into a life of semi-seclusion, preferring to keep your own counsel because others just don't seem to understand what you are trying to say.

The negative 7 lives in a world all of his own, preferring to romanticise and dream rather than face up to the realities of life. He should learn to understand that not all things can be, as in our dreams, a perfect match.

Your numbers vibrate to the planets Sun, Venus and Neptune.

As a 16/7 you are artistic, creative and versatile. You have a vivid imagination that you can, if you desire, put to constructive use. You are a lover of all that is beautiful and graceful in life. You are a far-seeing dreamer who forms the basis of changes within society. You can at times be unorthodox in your approach to everyday life. You can be both a mother and father to your children, and often are. You would make a great arbitrator, being able to see both sides of a dispute. Your creativity, if un-suppressed, would make you a great fashion designer or architect of new modern dwelling places.

In partnerships you are not all that you appear to be, having hidden depths of emotional feeling that are quickly or easily aroused. You require a very loving and understanding mate who gives stability to your ideals.

As a negative 16/7 your emotional sensitivity and creativity run riot. You imagine that all around you disasters are about to occur, and would have filled a Noah's Ark years before the flood ever happened, just in case.

You demand great loyalty and reassurance from your chosen mate, to such an extent that you can squeeze any emotional relationships dry. You must learn to separate dreams and subconscious fears from reality. You must develop a more open and understanding relationship with your chosen mate and discuss your fears, worries and anxieties with him or her in order that they may be dealt with for what they are.

Your birth number is 16/7

Name: Date of birth:

Lucky number: Lucky colour:

Partner's birth number:

Positive characteristics:

Negative characteristics:

Your birth number is
17/8

Your lucky numbers are: 8, 17, 26, 35, 44, 53, 63, 71, 80, 89, 98.
Your lucky colours are: black and all dark shades, such as burgundy.
Your best partners are: other 8s, 4s or 1s.

Your character

As a ruling 8 person you are a materialist. People born under this vibration have great business heads and management ability. They prefer things they can measure or see in a real way and scoff at the dreamers. They make great bankers, lawyers, stock brokers, etc. They love a challenge and their ability to wait for the right moment usually sees them in the top jobs and positions of their chosen careers. They don't like losers.

Many politicians vibrate to an 8 as they achieve success in their business and seek out new challenges to tax their managerial ability.

The negative 8 on the other hand is out of touch with reality, always wanting to start at the top of his chosen field without realising that he may have the ability but not the experience.

Your numbers vibrate to the planets Sun, Neptune and Saturn.

As a 17/8 you are sharp, shrewd and imaginative with the ability to make constructive use of the world of commerce. You are both a dreamer and a doer as you put your dreams into hard reality or stop having such dreams. You have the luck of the devil, as no matter how close you get to the edge of a cliff you always find somewhere firm to plant your feet. This birth number brings its bearer wealth and material success of one form or another.

You have found the secret of separating business and pleasure. You work hard at projects but know how to take time off to enjoy the rewards of your toils. You are able to enjoy your work and be stress-free in play.

In partnerships or romance you are quite content with an average body but prefer a stimulating mind with which to pass your periods of relaxation. Many self-made business men are born under this vibration.

As a negative 17/8 you become a materialist with no time for frivolities such as play. You become preoccupied with attaining security through the material plane, and though you may find riches, you will rarely find happiness.

Your mate is kept on a shoestring budget and you will be considered mean or miserly by your friends and neighbours, that is if you trust anyone enough to call them a friend. You must learn to unwind and share with others. You must realise that though we live in a material world there is a spiritual one parallel to it which we cannot ignore to the detriment of our karma. You were gifted in life in order that you may assist others as well.

Your birth number is $17/8$

Name: Date of birth:

Lucky number: Lucky colour:

Partner's birth number:

Positive characteristics:

Negative characteristics:

Your birth number is
18/9

Your lucky numbers are: 9, 18, 27, 36, 45, 54, 63, 72, 81, 90, 99.
Your lucky colours are: scarlet, red and orange.
Your best partners are: other 9s, 3s or 5s.

Your character
As a ruling 9 person you are supercharged full of energy, vitality and the will to achieve great things. On the positive side you are a workaholic, your energies never ebb and you have to keep yourself constantly on the move. It would not suit you to work where you have no freedom of self-expression as you are an extrovert who likes to do well and has no time for the inept or slow-witted.

Many 9s prefer to work for themselves as they do not get on well with employers' rules that do not fit in with their lifestyles. They are adventurous and will be involved with most risk sports or ventures, thriving on excitement. They should be careful that they do not take on more than they can handle as they tend to be Jack of all trades and master of none. They tend to become bored easily and need to be kept on the boil if they are to achieve.

The negative 9 is a bit of an egomaniac; he can be very domineering, even to the extent of crushing those who oppose his ideals.

Your numbers vibrate to the planets Sun, Saturn and Mars.

As an 18/9 you are an industrialist full of energy and vitality to achieve that which you desire in life regardless of your birth environment. You both dream and expect great things in your life. You are more mature than your years and can become frustrated with your fellow man's inability to see you in terms of mental rather than physical maturity. You try for the top jobs and get them with your dogmatic approach. You can miss out on the fun side of life in earlier years, preferring to build the security from which you will later be able to enjoy life. In romance you prefer older or maturer partners who can conform with your plans. You have a tendency to be too serious and need to let your hair down a little more. Under stress, you will become irritable and impatient and it is this that will cause any problems on your path to the top.

As a negative 18/9 you are power hungry and feel that the whole world is against you. You try for jobs out of your depth and become angry when others do not see the genius that you believe you are made from. You wander from relationship to relationship, wondering why nobody understands your kind, sensitive nature, when you were, in fact, too concerned with yourself to notice the problems of your mate, which is why he or she looked elsewhere.

You need to take stock of yourself. You may have the inner ability to be the managing director, but before this responsibility is handed out, people want to see a proven track record, so learn to start at the bottom. If you follow this path, your abilities will soon be noted and your climb to the top should be swift. You must learn humility.

Your birth number is 18/9

Name: Date of birth:

Lucky number: Lucky colour:

Partner's birth number:

Positive characteristics:

Negative characteristics:

Your birth number is

19/1

Your lucky numbers are: 1, 10, 19, 28, 37, 46, 55, 64, 73, 82, 91, 100.
Your lucky colours are: crimson, flame and white.
Your best partners are: other 1s, 4s or 8s.

Your character
As a ruling 1 person you are the father of all numbers. It is the symbol of unity; it stands for ambition, originality, independence and firmness of purpose. Ruling 1s are born leaders. You are very original in thought and action, therefore very creative. You are explorers, pioneers, promoters and organisers. One as a birth number is quite forceful, tending to dominate the environment in which the individual operates.

A negative ruling 1 is arrogant, domineering, egotistical, inconsiderate and selfish, too concerned with his own life to notice the plight of others.

Your numbers vibrate to the planets Sun and Mars.

As a 19/1 you are at times a little too rash in your words, thoughts and actions. You can be the life and soul of the party, though you will leave for pastures new if you feel the host is neglecting you.

Your inherent leadership ability is a great asset to you, though you should first make sure that the people you are leading want to be led. You are prone to be brought before the public whether for good or bad.

19/1s would make great politicians, managers of large corporations or officers in armies. They should endeavour to take up a sport as they have more than their fair share of energy and need an outlet for the excess.

The negative 19/1 is concerned entirely with his own needs and desires. He respects only those stronger than himself and will allow no interference in his lifestyle. He will always find someone to blame if things go wrong.

A tendency to rush into things without first checking all the details involved could bring about your downfall. If you concentrate on the job in hand, you are bound to excel, whereas dissipation of energies causes failure.

Your birth number is ¹⁹/₁

Name: Date of birth:

Lucky number: Lucky colour:

Partner's birth number:

Positive characteristics:

Negative characteristics:

Your birth number is
20/2

Your lucky numbers are: 2, 11, 20, 29, 38, 47, 56, 65, 74, 83, 92.
Your lucky colours are: salmon, grey and navy blue.
Your best partners are: other 2s, 5s or 7s.

Your character

As a ruling 2 you stand for duality, sharing and partnership. You are deeply sensitive and feel a great need to share your thoughts and emotions with someone that you feel you can trust with your insecurities. The bonds that you form can become intense, blocking out all else in your life. All 2s are kind, gentle, preferring the peaceful path if at all possible, though they should be careful that others do not misuse this.

The greatest fault of 2s is that they can become too sensitive and timid, reacting to extremes of happiness and depression. You should cultivate a bit more of the 'get up and go' of the ruling 1.

Your numbers vibrate to the planet Moon.

As a 20/2 you are a little less forceful than your fellow man. Your birth number is a little less physical but a lot more imaginative and intuitive. You would make a good arbitrator, being able to see both sides of issues. The number represents partnerships which you require with every part of your being. You are emotionally very intense, needing a great deal of understanding, love and affection in your relationships.

You require a little more room to think when making important decisions as you tend to lack confidence in yourself and need more time for thought. If pushed into decisions, you tend to panic or worry too much.

Your number vibrates to the mother and you are very compassionate and caring and tend to spoil your offspring with love and affection. This is one of the parts of your life you will fight to protect.

As a negative 20/2 you are a bag of nerves, always fearing that the worst is going to happen, or already has. You become despondent and melancholy and retreat into your imagination which creates better lifestyles. You are the bringer of doom and gloom, always seeing the negative side of things and worrying that your life is falling apart. You need to grasp opportunities rather than fear the negative outcome of them. You must learn to put your gifts to good use in the fields of artistic, creative or caring modes. In doing so you will gain all the recognition, praise and reassurance that you crave so much.

Your birth number is 20/2

Name: Date of birth:

Lucky number: Lucky colour:

Partner's birth number:

Positive characteristics:

Negative characteristics:

Your birth number is
21/3

Your lucky numbers are: 3, 12, 21, 30, 39, 48, 57, 66, 75, 84, 93.
Your lucky colours are: purple, burgundy and black.
Your best partners are: other 3s, 6s and 9s.

Your character

As a ruling 3 person you are independent both in your mannerisms and speech. You are ultra-adaptable, being able to become the person required of the moment. You show artistic flair and ability and a vivid imagination. Your versatility is well known among your ever-increasing circle of friends.

Ruling 3s make great actors, poets, teachers and salesmen. They have a natural ability that enables them to pick things up very quickly. Their biggest fault is that they can at times spread themselves a bit thin on the ground, having too many balls in the air at one time. Should things go wrong, they need no sympathy from others; they generate their own.

Your numbers vibrate to the planets Moon, Sun and Jupiter.

As a 21/3 you were born with the ability to excel in almost anything you turn your hand at. You have the drive and personality backed by the Sun with the emotional understanding and intuition of the Moon. The two combined will work well in your favour through Jupiter, the great benefactor. You are a good mediator, master or worker and blend in with your environment. You are a fun seeker whose only enemy is boredom. You are well liked by those around you and your social diary is usually full. You will fight for the rights of the underdog and win the respect and admiration of your friends. You would be better advised not to settle down too soon as this would make you restless. You need to travel and see and do exciting things before you tie yourself down to the responsibilities of parenthood. You are an adoring parent who can spoil his children, wanting them to have all the things you feel you missed out on as a child. If you become bored, you will quickly move on to something new and exciting.

A negative 21/3 is that lovable devil whom you just can't help liking even though you don't always agree with what he is doing. You can take advantage of other people's willingness to forgive at times. You think that the grass is always greener on the other side, become bored easily with what you are doing and lack staying power in both work and emotional commitments. You must learn to do as you have promised. You tend to have double values: that which is right for you, and that which is right for others. Even a court jester can be beheaded if he annoys the king, so beware.

Your birth number is $^{21}/_3$

Name: Date of birth:

Lucky number: Lucky colour:

Partner's birth number:

Positive characteristics:

Negative characteristics:

Your birth number is

22/4

Your lucky numbers are: 4, 13, 22, 31, 40, 49, 58, 67, 76, 85.
Your lucky colours are: blue, green and indigo.
Your best partners are: other 4s, 1s or 8s.

Your character
As a positive ruling 4 you are a builder, both on the material and the intellectual planes, always busy mentally and physically. A 4 makes a splendid bookmaker or mechanic; he is mathematical, methodical, a master of detail and routine. He is a splendid builder of systems for greater economy. His ambitions are of a personal nature for his own self-development.

All 4s need a firm platform from which to operate. Once this is achieved they find themselves free from the worries and fears that held them back from their ideals and dreams in the first place. Go on, commit yourself.

As a negative 4 you are despondent, buried beneath adverse circumstances, financial limitations and hard work, a plodder without any desire for intellectual development.

Your numbers vibrate to the planets Moon and Uranus.

As a 22/4 you were born with one of the master numbers in numerology if used on its higher plane of existence. This birth number is able to blend the imagination and the practical into concrete reality. You are very industrious with a flair for solving the problems that mystify and thwart those around you. You are an extrovert, and though your ideas may appear to others a little hare-brained they are built upon firm concepts. You are one of the builders of society and your dreams, though at times appearing selfish, are for what you consider the betterment of your fellow man and his surroundings. You are a hard taskmaster in work routines.

In relationships you subconsciously seek one who is not only attractive but intelligent, as you aim for the top and don't want a mate who will slow you down in your ambitions. You can be a good sports person.

As a negative 22/4 you try to force your views and opinions upon those around you and although your ideals may be correct, your methods are not. You can attempt to take the law into your own hands and may be a nonconformist. Many terrorists have this birth vibration, opting for violent enforced change in society, being rebels against the majority. Your fight for the underdog can be taken to extremes. You must learn to conform with the majority.

As a 22/4 you were gifted with the ability to lead others from the strife of the world we know today. This is a democratic process, taking years or decades, not weeks or months. You must develop patience.

Your birth number is 22/4

Name: Date of birth:

Lucky number: Lucky colour:

Partner's birth number:

Positive characteristics:

Negative characteristics:

Your lucky numbers are: 5, 14, 23, 32, 41, 50, 59, 68, 77, 86, 95.
Your lucky colours are: scarlet, orange and wine.
Your best partners are: other 5s, 2s or 7s.

Your character
As a ruling 5 person you are a wanderer. Mental activity is strong with 5 people; they just don't seem able to find the neutral gear, are always full of bright ideas and projects. The number is sometimes called the freedom seeker, as the ruling 5 is always on the go, loves to travel and hates restrictions of any kind. Fives are best employed in a job that has few restrictions as they hate regulations. Quick-witted and with few inhibitions, these people are usually found in the positions of stress that others find difficult to control.

The negative 5, on the other hand, is the chatterbox who rants on endlessly and says very little, too preoccupied with his own ego and self-praise to notice that he is boring his friends. Ulcers and stress-orientated illnesses prevail and there can be a tendency to mental burn-outs which leave him dazed and disorientated.

Your numbers vibrate to the planets Moon, Jupiter and Mercury.

As a 23/5 you have the compassion of the Moon, coupled with the generosity of Jupiter; add the ability of Mercury for communications and we find a person who not only says that he will do something but will see that it is done. You are very caring and considerate of those around you, and your carefree, amicable outer shell makes it easy for you to mix in most social circles with the ease of a bird in the air. You would make an excellent diplomat.

You are born out of your time, or so it appears to you. Your dreams and ideals are advanced and you hate restrictions which stop you from accomplishing the job you are involved in. You are a little impatient. You take life at a pace that leaves your contemporaries huffing and puffing, and inactivity, both business and social, is the death of you. You can earn excellent money but tend to spend it just as quickly, and why not?

You are highly intuitive and, although you may scoff at fortune tellers, you would probably make a good one yourself. You can be overactive and need to let your hair down on occasion. Marriage is best left until later in life.

As a negative 23/5 the reverse is so. You don't wish to do the hard work and will use your intuition or cunning to get others to do your dirty work for you. You will have a chip on your shoulder against all in authority. You feel sorry for yourself and will try to live off the pity and generosity of those around you. You will be the public house braggart who was in many heroic actions, when in reality you never left the safety of home.

You must learn to do more and say a little less. People will respect the silent stranger more than the village idiot. You must control your over-active ego.

Your birth number is 23/5

Name: Date of birth:

Lucky number: Lucky colour:

Partner's birth number:

Positive characteristics:

Negative characteristics:

Your birth number is

24/6

Your lucky numbers are: 6, 15, 24, 33, 42, 51, 60, 69, 78, 87, 96.
Your lucky colours are: bitter chocolate, green and deep sea blue.
Your best partners are: other 6s, 9s and 3s.

Your character

As a ruling 6 person you are kind and gentle-hearted, generous and peaceful, striving constantly to put right other people's wrongs. You are known for your adoration of children and the beautiful, artistic things in life with which you try to surround yourself. You would make an excellent nurse or social worker and can see both sides of most coins.

You do like an active social life, though you need the knowledge that you have a safe, secure home to retreat to. You may be very house-proud as you like your surroundings to look pleasing and be admired by visitors.

You can, on the negative side, be very vain, always admiring your own accomplishments and expecting others to do the same. Your ardent love for the home and family can cause you to find it difficult to break away on your own.

Your numbers vibrate to the planets Moon, Uranus and Venus.

As a 24/6 you are blessed with the intuition of the Moon coupled with the genius of Uranus which finds its outlets through the grace of Venus. You are compassionate, caring and quite an emotional or artistic person.

Your second number is 4 which represents security, buildings, forts and foundations. Thus in your career you will usually opt for working for larger concerns or groups rather than for yourself. You will need to know that your monetary scales are constant in order that you can plan for the future. Your total number is a 6. This has endowed you with a little bit more poise and grace to accomplish your dreams.

The 24/6 is ideally the home builder. All 24/6s thrive on the old traditions of secure home family life and home entertainment. Though they do enjoy travel and nights out, there is no place like home for them. They are very faithful in partnerships and expect the same from their chosen mate. They would make great social workers, nurses, or people who care for others in any capacity. They make great mothers and fathers.

As a negative 24/6 the reverse is so. You fear commitments in partnerships, always thinking the worst is going to happen, which causes you to become either very shy or very selfish on the emotional plane.

Your fears and anxieties cause you to withdraw from involvements which can result in great loneliness. Learn to trust people a little more, their motives just may be in your interest. Dream a little less, do a little more.

Your birth number is 24/6

Name: Date of birth:

Lucky number: Lucky colour:

Partner's birth number:

Positive characteristics:

Negative characteristics:

Your birth number is

25/7

Your lucky numbers are: 7, 16, 25, 34, 43, 52, 61, 70, 79, 88 and 97.
Your lucky colours are: sky blue, silver and sea green.
Your best partners are: other 7s, 5s or 2s.

Your character

As a ruling 7 person you are highly intuitive, constantly gathering information on the mysteries of life but seldom talking about them. A deep thinker but not a great doer, you are seldom understood by others and tend to withdraw. Your inability to express the real you can often lead you into a life of semi-seclusion, preferring to keep your own counsel because others just don't seem to understand what you are trying to say.

The negative 7 lives in a world all of his own, preferring to romanticise and dream rather than face up to the realities of life. He should learn to understand that not all things can be, as in our dreams, a perfect match.

Your numbers vibrate to the planets Moon, Mercury and Neptune.

As a 25/7 you are blessed with the compassion of the Moon, the communicative abilities of Mercury and the artistic intuition of Neptune. A career in the arts or creative design of allied fields would suit you well.

You are extremely sensitive to the thoughts, words and actions of your fellow man, although you may at times find it hard to find an outlet for your own inner thoughts and emotions. You can at least draw upon a vivid imagination. You can, at times, have a tendency to wander off into a world all of your own when the ambitions and hopes that you are striving to achieve appear difficult to obtain. Persevere, use your intuition and you will win through.

You are more than able to enjoy and express yourself in social circles once you have overcome your adolescent shyness. You will, however, feel more comfortable around maturer figures in your teenage years.

As a negative 25/7 you can be the world's greatest worrier. If you cannot find something to worry about, then you will worry because you have nothing to worry about. The slightest ache or pain can become horrific in your mind's eye. You can become despondent, fearing that all hope of ever achieving anything in your life has passed you by and will only be able to exist on the sympathies of others. You may also be prone to telling and living fairy tales. You must learn to separate the imaginary from the realities of everyday life or you may find others avoid you and make your worst fears of being alone come true.

Your birth number is 25/7

Name: Date of birth:

Lucky number: Lucky colour:

Partner's birth number:

Positive characteristics:

Negative characteristics:

Your birth number is
26/8

Your lucky numbers are: 8, 17, 26, 35, 44, 53, 62, 71, 80, 89, 98.
Your lucky colours are: black and all dark shades, such as burgundy.
Your best partners are: other 8s, 4s or 1s.

Your character

As a ruling 8 person you are a materialist. People born under this vibration have great business heads and management ability. They prefer things they can measure or see in a real way and scoff at the dreamers. They make great bankers, lawyers, stock brokers, etc. They love a challenge and their ability to wait for the right moment usually sees them in the top jobs and positions of their chosen careers. They don't like losers.

Many politicians vibrate to an 8, as they achieve success in their business and seek out new challenges to tax their managerial ability.

The negative 8, on the other hand, is out of touch with reality, always wanting to start at the top of his chosen field without realising that he may have the ability but not the experience.

Your numbers vibrate to the planets Moon, Venus and Saturn.

As a 26/8 you are blessed with the compassion and intuition of the Moon, the beauty, grace and modesty of Venus, coupled with the steadfast maturity of Saturn – a real recipe for success.

You thrive on partnerships of a sure and long-lasting nature. You are very loyal to your chosen mate although you do need the reassurance of being told you are loved. You appreciate and endeavour to possess things of beauty.

There would appear to have been some trauma or unhappiness in your childhood that loaded responsibilities to do with the family on your then young shoulders and, although difficult for you, you coped. At times you have a tendency to withdraw from stressful situations and should guard against the tendency to find scapegoats for whatever is not perfect in your life. A 26/8 has the ability to put dreams into reality.

Although this birth number has strong family ties, it is not prone to have large families of its own. The Saturn rulerships of early childhood restrictions can make 26/8s great aunts and uncles, but they fear having an heir of their own.

As a negative 26/8 there is danger of isolation. Early stresses can force you to withdraw from commitments of an emotional type. You become too possessive and your fear of deceit can create it. You become a materialist. In order to attain security, you set out to achieve it on a material rather than on a spiritual plane of existence. This may make you wealthy, but it will rarely make you happy. You must learn to trust your fellow man a little more and learn to give for the sake of giving rather than in the hope of receiving. If you elevate your spiritual existence, you will win the respect and admiration of all.

Your birth number is 26/8

Name: Date of birth:

Lucky number: Lucky colour:

Partner's birth number:

Positive characteristics:

Negative characteristics:

Your birth number is
27/9

Your lucky numbers are: 9, 18, 27, 36, 45, 54, 63, 72, 81, 90, 99.
Your lucky colours are: scarlet, red and orange.
Your best partners are: other 9s, 3s or 6s.

Your character

As a ruling 9 person you are supercharged full of energy, vitality and the will to achieve great things. On the positive side, you are a workaholic; your energies never ebb and you have to keep yourself constantly on the move. It would not suit you to work where you have no freedom of self-expression as you are an extrovert who likes to do well and has no time for the inept or slow-witted.

Many 9s prefer to work for themselves as they do not get on well with employers' rules that do not fit in with their lifestyles. They are adventurous and will be involved in most risk sports or ventures, thriving on excitement. They should be careful that they do not take on more than they can handle as they tend to be Jack of all trades and master of none. They tend to become bored easily and need to be kept on the boil if they are to achieve.

The negative 9 is a bit of an egomaniac. He can be domineering, even to the extent of crushing those who oppose his ideals.

Your numbers vibrate to the planets Moon, Mars and Neptune.

As a 27/9 you are gifted with the intuition and compassion of the Moon, the creativity and insight of Neptune and the aggressive push and energy of Mars. This can be a volatile mixture and would require some control.

This birth number fluctuates between the passive femininity of the 2 and 7 and the aggressive masculinity of the 9. There is, therefore, no emotional balance and extremes of happiness, depression, love and hate can be encountered. This birth number requires an understanding mate who can give a secure and stable home life and yet at the same time allow the freedom of expression and independence that they both require and demand. These 27/9 people are rarely what they seem on the outside. Their hard outer shell hides a heart of gold and if you ever win their trust, you have a friend for life, whereas their scorn is like Mount Etna in full eruption.

These people have gifted artistic or musical ability if they can ever tie themselves down for long enough to learn the notes, and this would tend to affect most things in their lives. They must learn patience. The negative 27/9 will flit from party to party nearly as quickly as from partner to partner. Insecurity prevents 27/9s from committing themselves to long-term relationships. They require constant attention. It's not that they are all bad when they are bad, it's just that their exterior attitude can be rather bombastic which does not tend to bring out the best in those around them. They must learn to show their true feelings.

Your birth number is 27/9

Name: Date of birth:

Lucky number: Lucky colour:

Partner's birth number:

Positive characteristics:

Negative characteristics:

CHRIS

> # *Your birth number is*
> # **28/10**

Your lucky numbers are: 1, 10, 19, 28, 37, 46, 55, 64, 73, 82, 91, 100.
Your lucky colours are: crimson, flame and white.
Your best partners are: **other 1s, 4s or 8s.**

Your character

As a ruling 1 person you are the father of all numbers. It is the symbol of unity; it stands for ambition, originality, independence and firmness of purpose. Ruling ones are born leaders. You are very original in thought and action, therefore very creative. You are explorers, pioneers, promoters and organisers. One as a birth number is quite forceful, tending to dominate the environment in which the individual operates.

A negative ruling 1 is arrogant, domineering, egotistical, inconsiderate and selfish, too concerned with his own life to notice the plight of others.

Your numbers vibrate to the planets Moon, Saturn and Sun.

As a 28/1 you are blessed with the intuition and compassion of the Moon, the maturity and business skills of Saturn and the magnetic aura of the Sun. People with this birth number can become leaders in politics and commerce. This birth number excels in the competitive market fields. Ones tend to give orders rather than take them and therefore usually attain some position of authority in relation to their careers.

In romance they are extremely protective and possessive and, although they can flirt, they desire only one true mate and expect the same in return. They make very proud, though quite strict, parents.

As a negative 28/1 you are a materialist, too concerned with your own well-being to think about the plight of your fellow men. You need to develop your sub-number 2 qualities of compassion and caring. Not everyone that you come into contact with is psychic enough to realise that you do not mean all the hard things that you sometimes say, so learn to treat your fellow men how you would have them treat you.

Your birth number is $^{28}/_{10}$

Name: Date of birth:

Lucky number: Lucky colour:

Partner's birth number:

Positive characteristics:

Negative characteristics:

Your lucky numbers are: 2, 11, 20, 29, 38, 47, 56, 65, 74, 83, 92.
Your lucky colours are: salmon, grey and navy blue.
Your best partners are: other 2s, 5s or 7s.

Your character

As a ruling 2 you stand for duality, sharing and partnership. You are deeply sensitive and find a great need to share your thoughts and emotions with someone that you feel you can trust with your insecurities. The bonds that you form can become intense, blocking out all else in your life. All 2s are gentle and kind, preferring the peaceful path if at all possible, though they should be careful that others do not misuse this.

The greatest fault of 2's is that they can become too sensitive and timid, reacting to extremes of happiness and depression. They should cultivate a bit more of the 'get up and go' of the ruling 1.

Your numbers vibrate to the planets Moon and Mars.

As a 29/2 you are blessed with the compassion, caring sensitivity of the Moon, coupled with the drive, energy and enthusiasm of Mars. People born with this combination of numbers are easily or quickly roused.

This vibration is either very masculine or very feminine. You will be very caring and sensitive, yet on the other hand very reactive to emotional situations. In romance you are very possessive, which can cause disputes.

You find it difficult, for some unknown reason, to express your inner emotions as they really are. You may feel like crying at times yet flare up like a sun gone nova to hide your real feelings. You are intensely caring and for you to give less than your all is unheard of. You will, however, find that as time goes by the rash, impulsive person you were mellows and, like a good wine, you get better with age.

As a negative 29/2 you allow your inner insecury to take over to the detriment of all else in your life. You can move from being elated one minute to being totally depressed the next. You must seek a happy medium. You were born with a sensitivity of emotion beyond belief; find a lost cause or redirect your intensity into your own insecurities and you will find that life is more than worth living. Learn to talk openly with loved ones.

Your birth number is $^{29}/_{11}$

Name: Date of birth:

Lucky number: Lucky colour:

Partner's birth number:

Positive characteristics:

Negative characteristics:

Your birth number is
30/3

Your lucky numbers are: 3, 12, 21, 30, 39, 48, 57, 66, 75, 84, 93.
Your lucky colours are: purple, burgundy and black.
Your best partners are: other 3s, 6s and 9s.

Your character
As a ruling 3 person you are independent both in your mannerisms and speech. You are ultra-adaptable, being able to become
the person required of the moment. You show artistic flair and
ability and have a vivid imagination. Your versatility is well
known among your ever-increasing circle of friends.

Ruling 3s make great actors, poets, teachers and salesmen. They
have a natural ability that enables them to pick things up
very quickly. Their biggest fault is that they can at times spread
themselves a bit thin on the ground, having too many balls in the
air at one time. Should things go wrong, they need no sympathy
from others; they generate their own.

Your numbers vibrate to the planet Jupiter.

As a 30/3 person you are philosophical, a good communicator
and a competent public speaker. You are generous to extremes at
times and always try to look on the bright side of life. Your
presence can bring life to dull parties. You can at times annoy
others as they feel that you do not take life seriously enough.
Although you are quite intelligent, you probably left school earlier
in life to explore the great unknown or travel overseas.

You are quite philosophical at times, wondering about the
mysteries of life and trying to solve the riddles of the unknown.
You can also be a practical joker, and would need to be watched
on April Fools Day.

A negative 30/3 does not want to take the responsibility for its actions, words or deeds. It prefers to think that life is one big merry-go-round and that problems will disappear if you ignore them. They need to learn that you have to be serious at some time in your life.

A firm commitment to a long-term project should teach them the patience that they lack in their everyday lives.

Your birth number is 30/3

Name: Date of birth:

Lucky number: Lucky colour:

Partner's birth number:

Positive characteristics:

Negative characteristics:

Your birth number is
31/4

Your lucky numbers are: 4, 13, 22, 31, 40, 49, 58, 67, 76, 85, 94.
Your lucky colours are: blue, green and indigo.
Your best partners are: other 4s, 1s or 8s.

Your character

As a positive ruling 4, you are a builder, both on the material and the intellectual planes, always busy mentally and physically. A 4 makes a splendid bookmaker or mechanic; he is mathematical, methodical, a master of detail and routine. He is a splendid builder of systems for greater economy. His ambitions are of a personal nature for his own self-development.

All 4s need a firm platform from which to operate. Once this is achieved they find themselves free from the worries and fears that held them back from their ideals and dreams in the first place. Go on, commit yourself.

As a negative 4 you are despondent, buried beneath adverse circumstances, financial limitations and hard work, a plodder without any desire for intellectual development.

Your numbers vibrate to the planets Jupiter, Sun and Uranus.

As a 31/4 you are outwardly fun-loving and quite extrovert. This is, however, not entirely the case. You do enjoy a good time and a night out on the town, but only if you think you have the spare cash to do so. In reality you are a secret worrier who can bottle up fears and anxieties and become at times explosive in emotional situations if you feel your partner is not showing the correct attitudes in your relationship. You need to learn not always to expect the worst to happen as in dreading the worst, or in over-testing, you often create that which you most fear can happen.

As a negative 31/4 you will constantly be on your guard against the things that could happen but probably never will anyway. You will want others to commit themselves to you first in order that you can trust them. You must learn to practise what you expect from others. They just may be waiting for that same commitment from you. If you act with a brash mannerism you can only expect others to treat you so.

Your birth number is ³¼

Name: Date of birth:

Lucky number: Lucky colour:

Partner's birth number:

Positive characteristics:

Negative characteristics:

Your birth number is
32/5

Your lucky numbers are: 5, 14, 23, 32, 41, 50, 59, 68, 77, 86, 95.
Your lucky colours are: scarlet, orange and wine.
Your best partners are: other 5s, 2s or 7s.

Your character

As a ruling 5 person you are a wanderer. Mental activity is strong with these people; they don't just seem to be able to find the neutral gear as far as mental activity is concerned, always full of bright ideas and projects. The number is sometimes called the freedom seeker, as the ruling 5 is always on the go, loves to travel and hates restrictions of any kind. Fives are best employed in a job that has few restrictions as they hate regulations. Quick-witted and with few inhibitions, these people are usually found in the positions of stress that others find difficult to control.

The negative 5 on the other hand is the chatterbox who rants on endlessly and says very little, too preoccupied with his own ego and self-praise to notice that he is boring the pants off his friends. Ulcers or stress-orientated illnesses prevail and there can be a tendency to mental burn-outs which leave him dazed and disorientated.

Your numbers vibrate to the planets Jupiter, Moon and Mercury.

As a 32/5 you are a hive of mental activity, always on the go, you find it very hard to unwind. If there is a job to be done, you will not be able to rest until it is accomplished. You are a workaholic who just can't rest. You are at times very impatient, not realising that not everyone has the same quick, astute mind or motives that you have to accomplish the job in hand. You are a freedom seeker who hates restrictions of any kind.

You are a bit of a wanderer, becoming bored with the same old routine all the time which causes you many changes of home or work, or you could be constantly redecorating to change the look of your environment.

You are at your best in stressful situations where you seem to excel. You do, however, seek the approval of others on completion of a project, though you will allow no criticism during it, as you are self-critical to extremes.

As a negative 32/5 you can misuse your sharp mind and fool yourself into believing your own fairy-tales. Ego and self-praise become the focal points in your life and you can become violent to that which you fear.

Your birth number is $^{32}/_5$

Name: Date of birth:

Lucky number: Lucky colour:

Partner's birth number:

Positive characteristics:

Negative characteristics:

Your lucky numbers are: 6, 15, 24, 33, 42, 51, 60, 69, 78, 87, 96.
Your lucky colours are: bitter chocolate, green and deep sea blue.
Your best partners are: other 6s, 9s and 3s.

Your character

As a ruling 6 person you are kind and gentle-hearted, generous and peaceful, striving constantly to put right other people's wrongs. You are known for your adoration of children and the beautiful, artistic things in life with which you try to surround yourself. You would make an excellent nurse or social worker and can see both sides of most coins.

You do like an active social life though you need the knowledge that you have a safe, secure home to retreat to. You may be very house-proud as you like your surroundings to look pleasing and be admired by visitors.

You can, on the negative side, be very vain, always admiring your own accomplishments and expecting others to do the same. Your ardent love for the home and family can cause you to find it difficult to break away on your own.

Your numbers vibrate to the planets Jupiter and Venus.

As a 33/6 you have for a birth number one of the master numbers. Few people actually act on the higher vibration of the 33 as it is the number of the saviour. Most work through the lower vibration of the 6. The birth number on the positive side is caring and compassionate and many people involved with the welfare of others, such as nurses, social workers and policemen, have this birth vibration. Women with this birth number are great mothers and usually go in for larger families, though this is not always the case.

A 33/6 can be quickly aroused on the emotional plane and should develop an ability to detach themselves from the rights or wrongs of other peoples' lifestyles. Such people can, if developed, make excellent arbitrators. They do have a deep need to be understood by others and can at times go to extremes in order to achieve this. They would require an understanding partner who is able to give in rather than argue in disputes.

On the negative side they can become power crazy, trying to enforce the changes that they believe to be for the better of all. The negative 33/6 would destroy rather than share that which he considered you should not have.

Your birth number is 33/6

Name: Date of birth:

Lucky number: Lucky colour:

Partner's birth number:

Positive characteristics:

Negative characteristics:

Your birth number is
34/7

Your lucky numbers are: 7, 16, 25, 34, 43, 52, 61, 70, 79, 88, 97.
Your lucky colours are: sky blue, silver and sea green.
Your best partners in life are: other 7s, 5s or 2s.

Your character
As a ruling 7 person you are highly intuitive, constantly gathering information on the mysteries of life but seldom talking about them. A deep thinker but not a great doer, you are seldom understood by others and tend to withdraw. Your inability to express the real you can often lead you into a life of semi-seclusion, preferring to keep your own counsel because others just don't seem to understand what you are trying to say.

The negative 7 lives in a world all of his own, preferring to romanticise and dream rather than to face up to the realities of life. He should learn to understand that not all things can be as in our dreams, a perfect match.

Your numbers vibrate to the planets Jupiter, Uranus and Neptune.

As a 34/7 you project a carefree and fun-loving exterior. This, however, is not the real you. You are, in fact, very sensitive and shy, reacting internally to all that is said or done in your presence. You need constant reassurance. This birth number does not like HP as they prefer to know what is theirs is theirs and cannot be taken from them. They will in marriage be very loyal, loving and caring, preferring to take on the submissive role. They make excellent mothers, even to the verge of spoiling their children. They do require to feel that they are wanted and needed, and will soon let you know if you are neglecting them. They are quite artistic and intuitive.

A negative 34/7, on the other hand, is always in dread that their world is going to tumble down about their ears. This causes them to subconsciously test the loyalty of those around them, which leads to quarrels. If you look for cracks in a wall long enough, you will find them. Then you will no longer trust that wall; so it is with relationships. You can create mistrust by fear of it.

You must learn to express your insecurities and expect others to just know that you are there. If you share a problem, it is said to be halved. People will not think you as silly as you think they would.

Your birth number is $^{34}/_7$

Name: Date of birth:

Lucky number: Lucky colour:

Partner's birth number:

Positive characteristics:

Negative characteristics:

Your birth number is
35/8

Your lucky numbers are: 8, 17, 26, 35, 44, 53, 62, 71, 80, 89, 98.
Your lucky colours are: black and all dark shades, such as burgundy.
Your best partners are: other 8s, 4s or 1s.

Your character
As a ruling 8 person you are a materialist. People born under this vibration have great business heads and management ability. They prefer things they can measure or see in a real way. They scoff at dreamers. They make great bankers, lawyers, stock brokers, etc. They love a challenge and their ability to wait for the right moment usually sees them in the top jobs and positions of their chosen careers. They don't like losers.

Many politicians vibrate to an 8, as they achieve success in their business and seek out new challenges to tax their managerial ability.

The negative 8, on the other hand, is out of touch with reality, always wanting to start at the top of his chosen field without realising that he may have the ability but not the experience.

Your numbers vibrate to the planets Jupiter, Mercury and Saturn.

As a 35/8 you are sensible, cautious and serious. You find it quite hard to enjoy yourself unless you feel that your work for the day is complete. You are mature before your years and seek to achieve material security. You find the company of older people more stimulating in your younger years because you find them more responsible. You can be a bit of a stick in the mud with people of your own age-group as you find them a little immature. You must try to enjoy yourself when younger as you may have more money or stability when a little older, but perhaps not the energy of youth to enjoy it. You will relate to a bird in the hand rather than two in the bush.

You must learn to take life as it comes and realise that you cannot go through life expecting everything to work out just as you planned. You must endeavour to treat others a little less like the machine that you are at times.

As a negative 35/8 you allow the need for material security to become an obsession that turns into greed. You expect others to be as efficient as you are, not realising that they are not up to your standard. You must endeavour to let your hair down from time to time after periods of hard work. The disco may not be your scene, but a night at the theatre could be.

Your birth number is ³⁵⁄₈

Name: Date of birth:

Lucky number: Lucky colour:

Partner's birth number:

Positive characteristics:

Negative characteristics:

Your lucky numbers are: 9, 18, 27, 36, 45, 54, 63, 72, 81, 90, 99.
Your lucky colours are: scarlet, red and orange.
Your best partners are: other 9s, 3s or 5s.

Your character
As a ruling 9 person you are supercharged full of energy, vitality and the will to achieve great things. On the positive side you are a workaholic, your energies never ebb and you have to keep yourself constantly on the move. It would not suit you to work where you had no freedom of self-expression as you are an extrovert who likes to do well and has no time for the inept or slow-witted.

Many 9s prefer to work for themselves as they do not get on well with employers' rules that do not fit in with their lifestyles. They are adventurous and are involved in most risk sports or ventures, thriving on excitement. They should be careful that they do not take on more than they can handle as they tend to be Jack of all trades and master of none. They tend to become bored easily and need to be kept on the boil if they are to achieve.

The negative 9 is a bit of an egomaniac. He can be very domineering even to the extent of crushing those who oppose his ideals.

Your numbers vibrate to the planets Jupiter, Venus and Mars.

As a 36/9 you are blessed with the beauty and grace of Venus coupled with the philosophy of Jupiter and the drive and ambition of Mars, a more than adequate combination for success in your chosen lifestyle. You are friendly, optimistic and sympathetic, a good mediator in family disputes with a magnetic aura that seems to draw the other sex with ease. You need to accomplish security on a material level.

Positive and constructive, you will endeavour to reach for the clouds and, with the energy of Mars, achieve just that in the long term. You need to curb the impulse to do too much in too short a time. Planning has its good points. You will need to ensure that your desire for comfort and security do not interfere with your impatience for achieving everything in the shortest time possible. If you have one more partner than you need, you may get found out.

As a negative 36/9 you will be rash, impulsive and possess very little patience for others or their problems, being too concerned with what you consider will better your own ideals or lifestyle.

You will become obsessed with the projection and notoriety of your own accomplishments, always finding excuses for your inability to blend with your fellow man. You will be lazy, only wanting to work when it suits you. You must learn to subdue your feelings of inadequacy that drive you into stressful and incomplete relationships, desiring others to take care of your problems, but under your terms.

Your birth number is 36/9

Name: Date of birth:

Lucky number: Lucky colour:

Partner's birth number:

Positive characteristics:

Negative characteristics:

59

Your birth number is
37/10

Your lucky numbers are: 1, 10, 19, 28, 37, 46, 55, 64, 73, 82, 91, 100.
Your lucky colours are: crimson, flame and white.
Your best partners are: other 1s, 4s or 8s.

Your character

As a ruling 1 person you are the father of all numbers. It is the symbol of unity; it stands for ambition, originality, independence and firmness of purpose. Ruling 1s are born leaders. You are very original in thought and action, therefore very creative. You are explorers, pioneers, organisers and promoters. One as a birth number is quite forceful, tending to dominate the environment in which the individual operates.

A negative ruling 1 is arrogant, domineering, egotistical, inconsiderate and selfish, too concerned with his own life to notice the plight of others.

Your numbers vibrate to the planets Jupiter, Neptune and Sun.

As a 37/1 you are idealistic, generous and hospitable and yet not always practical enough to implement your charitable ideals. You can be very intuitive, even psychic, with which you can inspire others to greater things. You can, at times, be absent-minded, too wrapped up in your dreams or thoughts to notice what is transpiring around you. You may find yourself attracted to cults or unusual group activities with which you feel an affinity. You are deeply sensitive to the thoughts and actions of those around you, although you find it difficult to express the real you to them. You will be very stubborn and have been known to bite off your nose to spite your face.

As a negative 37/1 you will resent the need to grow up and resist it with all the will of your imagination. You will feel safe and secure only in the childish fantasies that your mind creates to escape realities. The 37/1 person has a lot going for him if only he could project his ideas for the future in concrete form. He needs to learn that fairy-tales rarely come true or have happy endings in reality.

If you stop hoping that the best will come through in the end, then the worst will never happen, as it is only your fear of it that creates it. You cannot be either happy or sad. Find a balance between the two.

Your birth number is $^{37}/_{10}$

Name: Date of birth:

Lucky number: Lucky colour:

Partner's birth number:

Positive characteristics:

Negative characteristics:

Sonja.

Your birth number is
38/11

Your lucky numbers are: 2, 11, 20, 29, 38, 47, 56, 65, 74, 83, 92.
Your lucky colours are: salmon, grey and navy blue.
Your best partners are: other 2s, 5s or 7s.

Your character
As a ruling 2 you stand for duality, sharing and partnership. You are deeply sensitive and find a great need to share your thoughts and emotions with someone that you feel you can trust with your insecurities. The bonds that you form can become intense, blocking out all else in your life. All 2s are gentle and kind, preferring the peaceful path if at all possible though they should be careful that others do not misuse this.

The greatest fault of 2s is that they can become too sensitive and timid, reacting to extremes of happiness and depression. They should cultivate a bit more of the 'get up and go' of the ruling 1.

Your numbers vibrate to the planets Jupiter, Saturn and Moon.

As a 38/2 you are mothers of society, deeply sensitive to the environment or well-being of your fellow man. You would make a great nurse or social worker, civil servant or famine relief agent.

You have both the caring and generosity of Jupiter coupled with the maturity of Saturn which enables you to put your ideals into concrete reality. In marriage or partnerships you are very loyal and expect the same in return. You may not always show your real feelings on the surface and can at times be swept up by the emotional tide of your environment, realising too late that it is out of your control. Learn to be a little firmer.

As a negative 38/2 you are too sensitive to other people. You can take offence at a chance remark, feeling it was a personal dig at you. You need to learn to listen with two ears and take things as they were meant. You can become obsessed with an idea to the detriment of all else, thus destroying all that was secure in your life. You need to talk things out more with your mate, but be honest about your feelings; not everyone is psychic.

Let the strong intuition and femininity that you possess become your guide in life and you will see how quickly problems are overcome and any obstacle conquered, because you will now have confidence in yourself.

Your birth number is $^{38}/_{11}$

Name: Date of birth:

Lucky number: Lucky colour:

Partner's birth number:

Positive characteristics:

Negative characteristics:

Your birth number is
39/12

Your lucky numbers are: 3, 12, 21, 30, 39, 48, 57, 66, 75, 84, 93.
Your lucky colours are: purple, burgundy and black.
Your best partners are: other 3s, 6s and 9s.

Your character

As a ruling 3 person you are independent both in your mannerisms and speech. You are ultra-adaptable, being able to become the
person required of the moment. You show artistic flair and ability
and a vivid imagination. Your versatility is well known among
your ever-increasing circle of friends.

Ruling 3s make great actors, poets, teachers and salesmen. They
have a natural ability that enables them to pick things up very
quickly. Their biggest fault is that they can at times spread themselves a bit thin on the ground, having too many balls in the air at
one time. Should things go wrong, they need no sympathy from
others; they generate their own.

Your numbers vibrate to the planets Jupiter and Mars.

As a 39/3 you are frank, honest and trustworthy, inspiring
confidence and respect in your fellow man. You possess a magnetic personality and are blessed with the ability to succeed in
your chosen career.

Energetic and forceful, you are a born leader who naturally
excels at whatever you try your hand at. You are at the front in the
fashion scene, wanting to try out the unusual or extrovert designs.

You are very intelligent, though you probably left school earlier
in life in order that you could experience all the wonders of the
world. You do tend at times to have too many irons in the fire,
which can cause minor burns.

A 39/3 will require an understanding mate as he is quite flirtatious and finds it difficult to tie himself down to just one partner. However, when he does, he is very loving and faithful.

As a negative 39/3 your sharp mind and energy can be put to great misuse. You can have scant regard for the law of the land and will undoubtedly be a teller of great big white lies which you will come to believe yourself. You will be quite unreliable in moments of stress and may even exert force to try to quell anything which you feel threatens your stability. You must learn to develop patience, as it will be your only escape from yourself.

A long-term investment in land or property should give you the basis on which to build and develop a better lifestyle free from the worries and insecurities of the negative side of your birth number.

Your birth number is ³⁹/₁₂

Name: Date of birth:

Lucky number: Lucky colour:

Partner's birth number:

Positive characteristics:

Negative characteristics:

Your lucky numbers are: 4, 13, 22, 31, 40, 49, 58, 67, 76, 85, 94.
Your lucky colours are: blue, green and indigo.
Your best partners are: other 4s, 1s or 8s.

Your character

As a positive ruling 4, you are a builder, both on the material and intellectual planes, always busy mentally and physically. A 4 makes a splendid bookmaker or mechanic; he is mathematical, methodical, a master of detail and routine. He is a splendid builder of systems for greater economy. His ambitions are of a personal nature for his own self-development. All 4s need a firm platform from which to operate. Once this is achieved they find themselves free from the worries and fears that held them back from their ideals and dreams in the first place. Go on, commit yourself.

As a negative 4, you are despondent, buried beneath adverse circumstances, financial limitations and hard work, a plodder without any desire for intellectual development.

Your numbers vibrate to the planet Uranus.

As a 40/4 you are considered to be a bit of a rebel. You have viewpoints that differ from those of the general majority. You are courteous and generous, but you are also very sensitive and easily hurt. Your unconventional views are often applied in social or political issues and you delight in positive action. You have a great sympathy for the underdog, but can become dogmatic or rigid in your viewpoints. You are seldom interested in wealth for wealth's sake and can both acquire it and spend it without a second thought. You are loyal to your chosen friends, though at times you can be too possessive. You are highly creative in thought and can become very depressed if you feel that you are finding no expression or outlet for your creativity. You need to learn to avoid these periods of self pity.

As a negative 40/4 you lack emotional stability, fluctuating between periods of great elation and happiness and great despondency and sorrow. You become possessive of all you own, feeling others will steal it. You will withdraw from the stresses of maintaining meaningful relationships, always fearing that the other person will not commit themselves to you in the way you require for long-term security.

You must learn to live more for today than for the maybes of tomorrow, to look less for ulterior motives that other people may have and put a little trust into relationships. You will be amazed at the results.

Your birth number is 40/4

Name: Date of birth:

Lucky number: Lucky colour:

Partner's birth number:

Positive characteristics:

Negative characteristics:

Your birth number is
41/5

Your lucky numbers are: 5, 14, 23, 32, 41, 50, 59, 68, 77, 86, 95.
Your lucky colours are: scarlet, orange and wine.
Your best partners are: with other 5s, 2s or 7s.

Your character
As a ruling 5 person you are a wanderer. Mental activity is strong with these people, they just don't seem able to find the neutral gear as far as mental activity is concerned, always full of bright ideas and projects. The number is sometimes called the freedom seeker, as the ruling 5 is always on the go, loves to travel and hates restrictions of any kind. Fives are best employed in a job that has few restrictions as they hate regulations. Quick-witted and with few inhibitions, these people are usually found in the positions of stress that others find difficult to control.

The negative 5, on the other hand, is the chatterbox who rants on endlessly and says very little, too preoccupied with his own ego and self-praise to notice that he is boring the pants off his friends. Ulcers and stress-orientated illnesses prevail and there can be a tendency to mental burn-outs which leave him dazed and disorientated.

Your numbers vibrate to the planets Uranus, Sun and Mercury.

As a 41/5 you are very adaptable, being able to rebound from the depths of despair to the heights of happiness in a very short period of time. Mentally keyed up, you crave all kinds of change and excitement. A dull routine can make you feel depressed, or even ill. You have the ability to make money quite easily through your own inventiveness and ideas. You are prepared to take the risks that others fear. You are a quick thinker with a shrewd, sharp mind which leaves any competition behind. This, however, can make you impatient with others who lack your qualities and always appear to be holding you back. Any blows or setbacks are quickly overcome with new ideas and projects; although at the time you are at an all-time low, this is soon forgotten.

As a negative 41/5 you are prone to living on your mental energy to such an extent that you will undergo periods of mental burn-out. This can lead to health disorders such as ulcers or mental breakdown. If used to its lowest level you can become too dogmatic in your views and ideals, accepting or tolerating neither interference nor criticism of your lifestyle. You may then become alienated from your fellow man. You must learn to be more tolerant and patient of those who do not possess the ability to make the instant decisions you do with such ease. You must try to show more of the feelings you suppress.

Your birth number is 41/5

Name: Date of birth:

Lucky number: Lucky colour:

Partner's birth number:

Positive characteristics:

Negative characteristics:

Your birth number is
42/6

Your lucky numbers are: 6, 15, 24, 33, 42, 51, 60, 69, 78, 87, 96.
Your lucky colours are: bitter chocolate, green and deep sea blue.
Your best partners are: other 6s, 9s or 8s.

Your character
As a ruling 6 person you are kind and gentle-hearted, generous and peaceful, striving constantly to put right other people's wrongs. You are known for your adoration of children and the beautiful artistic things in life with which you try to surround yourself. You would make an excellent nurse or social worker and can see both sides of most coins.

You do like an active social life though you need the knowledge that you have a safe, secure home to retreat to. You may be very house-proud as you like your surroundings to look beautiful and pleasing and be admired by visitors.

You can, on the negative side, be very vain, always admiring your own accomplishments and expecting others to do the same. Your ardent love for the home and family can cause you to find it difficult to break away on your own.

Your numbers vibrate to the planets Uranus, Moon and Venus.

As a 42/6 you are magnetic and much loved by all who know you. This birth number has more friends than most and certainly knows how to mix well with other people. You are idealistic, romantic and a lover of beauty and the arts. You are at times a little obstinate when it comes to achieving your own wishes and desires and will require a degree of comfort, or even luxury, in your surroundings or possessions. You hate discord of any kind. You are fairly easy-going and will put up with quite a lot in order to keep the peace. However, when roused you will endeavour to end the dispute in the shortest, sharpest way. You are usually very loyal to your chosen mate. You are at your best as the mother hen caring for her brood, though if aroused you can be emotional hell to live with. You can at times be led astray by others, though you are by no means a soft sell.

As a negative 42/6 you are not a very nice person to know. You lack confidence in all you do and can annoy friends and relatives with your constant request for help or sympathy that is uncalled for. You require reassurance. You may retreat from everyday life, fearing the consequences of your own decisions. You lack confidence in yourself but also question the ability of those who try to help you through your bad patches. You must learn to take each day as it comes rather than dread it as it approaches. If someone attempts to help you, don't drive them away with constant questioning of their motives. Learn to relax.

Your birth number is 42/6

Name: Date of birth:

Lucky number: Lucky colour:

Partner's birth number:

Positive characteristics:

Negative characteristics:

Your birth number is
43/7

Your lucky numbers are: 7, 16, 25, 34, 43, 52, 61, 70, 79, 88 and 97.
Your lucky colours are: sky blue, silver and sea green.
Your best partners are: other 7s, 5s or 2s.

Your character

As a ruling 7 person you are highly intuitive, constantly gathering information on the mysteries of life but seldom talking about them. A deep thinker but not a great doer, you are seldom understood by others and tend to withdraw. Your inability to express the real you can often lead you into a life of semi-seclusion, preferring to keep your own counsel because others just don't seem to understand what you are trying to say.

The negative 7 lives in a world all of his own, preferring to romanticise and dream rather than face up to the realities of life. He should learn to understand that not all things can be as in our dreams, a perfect match.

Your numbers vibrate to the planets Uranus, Jupiter and Neptune.

As a 49/7 you are a little restless at heart. Your outlook is philosophical and, while you require a home base, you do at the same time consider the world as a whole to be your home. You are imaginative and a deep thinker. You will have little regard for money or what it will buy, being more of the view that it is a means to an end and is nothing to be cried over. Many wealthy 43/7s donate large sums to charities or similar organisations.

You are a natural healer and very compassionate towards your fellow man. This birth number has different viewpoints and can become involved in unorthodox or new religious movements such as we see in society today. You may be a gifted psychic or just have a strong intuition. However it manifests itself, others will find your foresight uncanny at times. You have an affinity with water and the sea and may feel more at home around water.

As a negative 43/7 you may still be a visionary though you will tend to operate on the fears and worry side of life. You will be highly sensitive to the thoughts or actions of others, fearing that they plot against you. You will at times border on genius in your plans but lack the confidence to put them into action. You will be a dreamer – full stop – and must learn to project your ideas in order that they may become realities. You must learn to spend more time with adventurous people whose confidence could give you the confidence you lack. You must become attuned to the realities of the world we live in and help to improve it.

Your birth number is 43/7

Name: Date of birth:

Lucky number: Lucky colour:

Partner's birth number:

Positive characteristics:

Negative characteristics:

ED   X

Your birth number is
44/8

Your lucky numbers are: 8, 17, 26, 35, 44, 53, 62, 71, 80, 89, 98.
Your lucky colours are: black and all dark shades, such as burgundy.
Your best partners are: other 8s, 4s or 1s.

Your character
As a ruling 8 person you are a materialist. People born under this
vibration have great business heads and management ability.
They prefer things they can measure or see in a real way and scoff
at the dreamers. They make great bankers, lawyers, stock brokers,
etc. They love a challenge and their ability to wait for the right
moment usually sees them in the top jobs and positions of their
chosen careers. They don't like losers.

Many politicians vibrate to an 8, as they achieve success in their
business and seek out new challenges to tax their managerial
ability.

The negative 8, on the other hand, is out of touch with reality,
always wanting to start at the top of his chosen field without
realising that he may have the ability but not the experience.

Your numbers vibrate to the planets Uranus and Saturn.

As a 44/8 you are in a bit of a quandary as the number totters
between the spiritual and the material. On one side you possess
occult philosophy and leanings and on the other upheavals and
material needs and desires. You will succeed in long-term ventures and will have great faith in that which you can see or lay
your hands on. At the same time you will be trying to find
explanations for the sources of life that escape you. Knowledge
tends to come to these people as they grow older, coupled with

the understanding of how to use it. A 44/8 is nearly always to be found in the public eye. He is very ambitious and always gets there in the end. He is a great fighter for the underdog and many politicians have this birth number. It is the positive number of the law-maker and 44/8 people may be misunderstood as they ensure the foundations of society remain firm.

As a negative 44/8 the reverse is that danger of isolation comes because the individual comes into conflict with the law and rebels against all the things that we consider sacred in our society, an underworld gang leader, for example. He considers only his needs and desires above all else and if he is seen to be doing good, it is only a cover for ulterior motives. This birth number is very unlucky on its negative side. You must learn to mix more with your fellow man and share your inner feelings which you tend to suppress. You may not be the jet set, but you would certainly enjoy watching them.

Your birth number is 44/8

Name: Date of birth:

Lucky number: Lucky colour:

Partner's birth number:

Positive characteristics:

Negative characteristics:

Your birth number is
45/9

Your lucky numbers are: 9, 18, 27, 36, 45, 54, 63, 72, 81, 90, 99.
Your lucky colours are: scarlet, red and orange.
Your best partners are: other 9s, 3s or 6s.

Your character
As a ruling 9 person you are supercharged full of energy, vitality and the will to achieve great things. On the positive side you are a workaholic; your energies never ebb and you have to keep yourself constantly on the move. It would not suit you to work where you have no freedom of self-expression as you are an extrovert who likes to do well and has no time for the inept or slow-witted.

Many 9s prefer to work for themselves as they do not get on well with employers' rules that do not fit in with their lifestyles. They are adventurous and will be involved in most risk sports or ventures, thriving on excitement. They should be careful that they do not take on more than they can handle as they tend to be Jack of all trades and master of none. They tend to become bored easily and need to be kept on the boil if they are to achieve.

The negative 9 is a bit of an egomaniac; he can be very domineering even to the extent of crushing those who oppose his ideals.

Your numbers vibrate to the planets Uranus, Mercury and Mars.

As a 45/9 you are keenly perceptive at times, although often limited in your outlook. Your mind is quick and active though a little impatient, which can lead to heated discussions. You would, however, excel in communications. Unlike your friends and associates, you are seldom short of that reserve of energy to accomplish any task that you set your mind upon; you seem to find that bit of extra when you need it most. You feel a deep inner need to accomplish tasks of real importance. You probably periodically become irritable without realising that a feeling of inactivity is the root cause. You are self-assured and confident. You have the ability to assert yourself and take charge of a situation without arousing the anger of others. You are also good at improving and encouraging a team effort.

As a negative 45/9 you often find that what you are thinking or saying conflicts with what you actually do in practice. Sometimes you will respond to an innocent remark as if it were a criticism or an order. If you could learn to listen more without interruption you could be quick and clever and admired to your heart's content.

Early family background may have left you with a chip on your shoulder and you may find it hard to share. You must learn to be a little more diplomatic in your dealings with other people. They do not always show the same energy for a project as you because they do not have your incentives.

Your birth number is 45/9

Name: Date of birth:

Lucky number: Lucky colour:

Partner's birth number:

Positive characteristics:

Negative characteristics:

Wendy

Your birth number is
46/10

Your lucky numbers are: 10, 19, 28, 37, 46, 55, 64, 73, 82, 91, 100.
Your lucky colours are: crimson, flame and white.
Your best partners are: other 1s, 4s or 8s.

Your character

As a ruling 1 person you are the father of all numbers. It is the symbol of unity; it stands for ambition, originality, independence and firmness of purpose. Ruling 1s are born leaders. You are very original in thought and action, therefore very creative. You are explorers, pioneers, promoters and organisers. One as a birth number is quite forceful, tending to dominate the environment in which the individual operates.

A negative ruling 1 is arrogant, domineering, egotistical, inconsiderate and selfish, too concerned with his own life to notice the plight of others.

Your numbers vibrate to the planets Uranus, Venus and Sun.

As a 46/1 you are blessed with the inventiveness of Uranus, the beauty, grace and compassion of Venus, and the magnetic aura of the Sun. People born under these numbers are usually great organisers. You are a builder on the material plane, always striving to better your environment at home and work. Your skills as an organiser are an asset to any large business or corporation, though you tend to need praise for a job well done. You require a stable base from which to operate and, although you don't mind giving orders, you are not so good at taking them unless you respect the giver. You are compassionate, though you don't always show it outwardly.

In romance you are quite possessive and faithful, and you demand the same from your chosen mate. Children may be few but they are nearly always spoilt by this birth number. All ruling 1s attain positions of authority.

As a negative 46/1 you may be a bit of a dictator, as the desire for security can cause over-reaction to domestic situations. Your fear of what might happen is what puts those around you under stress – stop worrying. You need to learn to trust those around you a little more. History tells us that dictators who ruled by force all fell by revolt. Show your inner emotions a little more. You'll be surprised at others' reactions.

Your birth number is ⁴⁶/₁₀

Name: Date of birth:

Lucky number: Lucky colour:

Partner's birth number:

Positive characteristics:

Negative characteristics:

Your birth number is
47/11

Your lucky numbers are: 2, 11, 20, 29, 38, 47, 56, 65, 74, 83, 92.
Your lucky colours are: salmon, grey and navy blue.
Your best partners are: other 2s, 5s or 7s.

Your character
As a ruling 2 you stand for duality, sharing and partnership. You are deeply sensitive and find a great need to share your thoughts and emotions with someone that you feel you can trust with your insecurities. The bonds that you form can become intense, blocking out all else in your life. All 2s are gentle and kind, preferring the peaceful path if at all possible, though they should be careful that others do not misuse this.

The greatest fault of 2s is that they can become too sensitive and timid, reacting to extremes of happiness and depression. They should cultivate a bit more of the 'get up and go' of the ruling 1.

Your numbers vibrate to the planets Uranus, Neptune and Moon.

As a 47/2 you are blessed with the genius of Uranus, the intuition and insight of Neptune and the compassion and caring of the Moon. People born with this birth number make great nurses, social workers and care attendants. You are artistic, caring and kind and will always have a sympathetic ear for a friend in need. In romance you require a lot of touching and stroking; contact and reassurance are important to you. Others sense this in you.

People with this birth number make adoring parents, though there can be a tendency to domestic upheavals. This is caused by one partner's neglect of the emotional needs of the 47/2, resulting in a search elsewhere. This birth number has a strong intuition and/or psychic ability though it needs to separate imaginary fears from true premonitions. There may be a tendency to stress-orientated illnesses, e.g. ulcers.

As a negative 47/2 the imaginary fears and worries of what may happen predominate in the lifestyle. This can lead to a lonely life as the subject may withdraw from emotional commitment in case it should go wrong. His fear and uncertainty of what could happen makes him blame others for his own lack of emotional expression. He will live off the emotional generosity of anyone he can find to give him the sympathy.

Your birth number is $^{47}/_{11}$

Name: Date of birth:

Lucky number: Lucky colour:

Partner's birth number:

Positive characteristics:

Negative characteristics:

Your birth number is
48/12

Your lucky numbers are: 3, 12, 21, 39, 48, 57, 66, 75, 84, 93.
Your lucky colours are: purple, burgundy and black.
Your best partners are: other 3s, 6s and 9s.

Your character
As a ruling 3 person you are independent both in your mannerisms and speech. You are ultra-adaptable, being able to become
the person required of the moment. You show artistic flair and
ability and a vivid imagination. Your versatility is well known
among your ever-increasing circle of friends.

Ruling 3s make great actors, poets, teachers and salesmen. They
have a natural ability that enables them to pick things up
very quickly. Their biggest fault is that they can at times spread
themselves a bit thin on the ground, having too many balls in the
air at one time. Should things go wrong, they need no sympathy
from others; they generate their own.

Your numbers vibrate to the planets Uranus, Saturn, and Jupiter.

As a 48/3 you are blessed with the inspiration of Uranus, the
logic and patience of Saturn and the philosophic nature of Jupiter.
People born with this vibration are the stable, secure institutions
of society. You are cautious in your dealings with other people
and rarely make the same mistake twice. You treat others as they
treat you and will give new contacts the benefit of the doubt until
they are able to prove themselves. People born with this vibration
can turn their hands to most things, having the versatility to put

learning to practical use. Shop-owners, small businessmen and sales people are commonly born with this vibration. The desire of the number is to achieve material security while still enjoying the fun things of life. So they can work hard, but they do need time off to play. In romance they may appear flirtatious but are very faithful.

As a negative 48/3 you can flit from romance to romance or job to job, lacking the maturity of Saturn to turn the luck of Jupiter into firm ground from which to develop. You must endeavour to commit yourself fully to projects. If you fail to do so, you will be the child who never grew up and will one day wonder how you could be so old and have achieved so little. Your saviour is that the Saturnian influence grows stronger as you get older, which can bring changes in fortune after 45. Learn to grow up sooner and you will achieve sooner.

Your birth number is $^{48}/_{12}$

Name: Date of birth:

Lucky number: Lucky colour:

Partner's birth number:

Positive characteristics:

Negative characteristics:

Your birth number is
49/13

Your lucky numbers are: 4, 13, 22, 31, 40, 49, 58, 67, 76, 85, 94.
Your lucky colours are: blue, green and indigo.
Your best partners are: other 4s, 1s or 8s.

Your character
As a positive ruling 4 you are a builder, both on the material and the intellectual planes, always busy, mentally and physically. A 4 makes a splendid bookmaker or mechanic; he is mathematical, methodical, a master of routine and detail. He is a splendid builder of systems for greater economy. His ambitions are of a personal nature for his own self-development.

All 4s need a firm platform from which to operate. Once this is achieved they find themselves free from the worries and fears that held them back from their ideals and dreams in the first place. Go on, commit yourself.

As a negative 4 you are despondent, buried beneath adverse circumstances, financial limitations and hard work, a plodder without any desire for intellectual development.

Your numbers vibrate to the planets Uranus and Mars.

As a 49/4 you are blessed with the inspirational genius of Uranus, coupled with the energy, drive and enthusiasm of Mars. People born with this birth number are either very confident and self-assured or overly inhibited. This birth number is rarely fully understood by its fellow men. The outer core is quite energetic, forceful or warlike; this, however, hides the inner personality which is insecure, or at least bottles up its fears and anxieties. The birth number is a mixture of both masculine and feminine. The 4 in the number craves security and stability while the stronger 9 thrives on risks and adventure. A balance between the two must be found for inner peace. You may fluctuate between being completely rushed off your feet one minute to being inactive and bored the next. The karma or lesson of the number is to achieve a balance between the two. When at their best 4 people excel at most things, having the energy and compulsion to overcome any obstacles.

As a negative 49/4 you will be short-tempered with others, trusting and doing nothing that you do not want to do. You can become quarrelsome with your chosen mate, constantly testing his or her loyalty. You must learn to lay firm foundations from which you would be more than able to build the empire of which your dreams are made.

Your birth number is $^{49}/_{13}$

Name: Date of birth:

Lucky number: Lucky colour:

Partner's birth number:

Positive characteristics:

Negative characteristics:

Your birth number is
50/5

Your lucky numbers are: 5, 14, 23, 32, 41, 50, 59, 68, 77, 86, 95.
Your lucky colours are: scarlet, orange and wine.
Your best partners are: other 5s, 2s or 7s.

Your character

As a ruling 5 person you are a wanderer. Mental activity is strong with these people; they just don't seem able to find the neutral gear as far as mental activity is concerned, always full of bright ideas and projects. The number is sometimes called the freedom seeker, as the ruling 5 is always on the go. He loves to travel and hates restrictions of any kind. Fives are best employed in a job that has few restrictions as they hate regulations. Quick-witted and with few inhibitions, these people are usually found in the positions of stress that others find difficult to control.

The negative 5, on the other hand, is the chatterbox who rants on endlessly and says very little, too pre-occupied with his own ego and self-praise to notice that he is boring the pants off his friends. Ulcers or stress-orientated illnesses prevail and there can be a tendency to mental burn-outs which leave him dazed and disorientated.

Your numbers vibrate to the planet Mercury.

As a 50/5 you are blessed with the sharp mind and wit of Mercury raised to the power of ten. This is not an easy birth number to explain. It is the middle birth number of this century and partakes of all and yet none. The number is sensitive to the surroundings in which it finds itself and yet discontented with parts of it; it just can't lay its finger on what, though. It requires both security and yet total freedom to express itself. The mind is very sharp and, although at times sarcastic, it tries to bring out the best in those who come into contact with it. It is very sensitive and easily offended and yet never shows its true emotional state. The imagination and intuition are strengthened and yet it scoffs at that which it considers illogical. People with this birth number do make great researchers or statisticians. In romance they need personal freedom of action.

This birth number is a bringer of change to society; born out of its time, or with ideas that do not conform, it is seldom fully understood by its fellow man until the passing of time has shown its ideology to be true. If you were born with this birth vibration do not make any promises that you cannot keep. It is not that you do not keep your word; it is more likely that you will have moved on to newer and more exciting projects.

Your birth number is $^{50}/_5$

Name: Date of birth:

Lucky number: Lucky colour:

Partner's birth number:

Positive characteristics:

Negative characteristics:

Your birth number is
51/6

Your lucky numbers are: 6, 15, 24, 33, 42, 51, 60, 69, 78, 87, 96.
Your lucky colours are: bitter chocolate, green and deep sea blue.
Your best partners are: other 6s, 9s and 3s.

Your character
As a ruling 6 person you are kind and gentle-hearted, generous and peaceful, striving constantly to put right other people's wrongs. You are known for your adoration of children and the beautiful, artistic things in life with which you try to surround yourself. You would make an excellent nurse or social worker and can see both sides of most coins. You do like an active social life though you need the knowledge that you have a safe, secure home to retreat to. You may be very house-proud as you like your surroundings to look pleasing and be admired by visitors.

You can, on the negative side, be very vain, always admiring your own accomplishments and expecting others to do the same. Your ardent love for the home and family can cause you to find it difficult to break away on your own.

Your numbers vibrate to the planets Mercury, Sun and Venus.

As a 51/6 you are blessed with the sharp mind of Mercury, the magnetic aura of the Sun and the grace and artistic sensitivity of Venus. People born with this birth number are the actors of life and the world is their stage. There is something about a 51/6 that you just can't help liking. Such people tend to put their viewpoints in a forceful manner and although they can at times appear lazy, they will, when the need arises, work as hard as the next man.

There is artistic, poetic or musical ability and while this can be exceptional in some 51/6s, so can their vanity. If nobody praises them for a job well done, they are more than able to praise themselves. In romance they require a lot of attention and although outwardly flirtatious, they are in fact quite faithful when being admired. In women, this birth number can give larger than average families. This birth number does have strong family ties but usually travels away from the family place of birth. Many actors, singers and air hostesses have this birth number.

As a negative 51/6 your rash, impulsive temper, quick sharp tongue or vanity can bring about your downfall. You must remember that not everyone has your quick understanding or strengths, and make allowances. Just because you were born with the gift to express your imagination doesn't mean you can live an imaginary lifestyle. Only the chosen few make it to the top. Your notoriety is dependent upon your environment.

Your birth number is $51/6$

Name: Date of birth:

Lucky number: Lucky colour:

Partner's birth number:

Positive characteristics:

Negative characteristics:

Your birth number is
52/7

Your lucky numbers are: 7, 16, 25, 34, 43, 52, 61, 70, 79, 88, 97.
Your lucky colours are: sky blue, silver and sea green.
Your best partners are: other 7s, 5s or 2s.

Your character
As a ruling 7 person you are highly intuitive, constantly gathering information on the mysteries of life but seldom talking about them. A deep thinker but not a great doer, you are seldom understood by others and tend to withdraw. Your inability to express the real you can often lead you into a life of semi-seclusion, preferring to keep your own counsel because others just don't seem to understand what you are trying to say.

The negative 7 lives in a world all of his own, preferring to romanticise and dream rather than face up to the realities of life. He should learn to understand that not all things can be as in our dreams, a perfect match.

Your numbers vibrate to the planets Mercury, Moon and Neptune.

As a 52/7 you are blessed with the compassion and caring of the Moon, the sharp wit and versatility of Mercury and the imagination and insight of Neptune. People born under these numbers are extremely artistic and sensitive. They have a burning ambition to communicate their inner emotions. This can show itself in commercial or domestic situations, dependent upon hereditary environment. In romance or home life, these people are very emotionally intense, requiring a great deal of caring and attention which they also give in return. They can express their inner emotion with ease and grace.

On a commercial level, these people are able to express their imaginations through creative outlets such as fashion design or town planning. They often become involved in charities as they have strong, caring emotions. There can be a tendency to withdraw in earlier life, but once these people have rid themselves of the shyness that is inherent in their birth number they will live and love life to its full.

As a negative 52/7 you are trapped in unfortunate circumstances. You may find it difficult to separate the imaginary from the reality. Subconscious fears and anxieties leave you tongue-tied and frustrated. You can become overly shy and withdraw into the safer realms of your imagination. Learn to say what you feel and you will attract the respect of your peers for your honesty and determination.

Your birth number is 52/7

Name: Date of birth:

Lucky number: Lucky colour:

Partner's birth number:

Positive characteristics:

Negative characteristics:

Your lucky numbers are: 8, 17, 26, 35, 44, 53, 62, 71, 80, 89, 98.
Your lucky colours are: black, and all dark shades, such as burgundy.
Your best partners are: other 8s, 4s or 1s.

Your character
As a ruling 8 person you are a materialist. People born under this vibration have great business heads and management ability. They prefer things they can measure or see in a real way and scoff at the dreamers. They make great bankers, lawyers, stock brokers, etc. They love a challenge and their ability to wait for the right moment usually sees them in the top jobs and positions of their chosen careers. They don't like losers.

Many politicians vibrate to an 8 as they achieve success in their business and seek out new challenges to tax their managerial ability.

The negative 8, on the other hand, is out of touch with reality, always wanting to start at the top of his chosen field without realising that he may have the ability but not the experience.

Your numbers vibrate to the planets Mercury, Jupiter and Saturn.

As a 53/8 you are blessed with the sharp mind and wit of Mercury, the big heart and philosophy of Jupiter and the maturity of Saturn. People born with this combination of numbers mature younger but enjoy life later. You are wise before your years and will travel away from your hereditary place of birth. Responsibilities come in younger years and your progress and promotion at work can be speedy. You are at times very logical and methodical.

You should avoid emotional commitments in your younger years as it can backfire on you in your mid-thirties. You need a firm material base from which to operate. Once this is achieved you are able to paint the town red. I believe the adage 'life begins at forty' was written for this birth number as by this age most have shed any material inhibitions and are able to live life to the full. Some can even experience a second childhood.

As a negative 53/8 you can become a complete materialist, wanting wealth and power for the sake of it. There is a danger of isolation from your fellow man. Many an eccentric millionaire has this type of birth vibration. You must learn to put your Saturn to constructive use. Responsibility was given in order that you could assist your fellow man, not just yourself.

Your birth number is 53/8

Name: Date of birth:

Lucky number: Lucky colour:

Partner's birth number:

Positive characteristics:

Negative characteristics:

Your birth number is
54/9

Your lucky numbers are: 9, 18, 27, 36, 45, 54, 63, 72, 81, 90, 99.
Your lucky colours are: scarlet, red and orange.
Your best partners are: other 9s, 3s or 6s.

Your character
As a ruling 9 person you are supercharged full of energy, vitality and the will to achieve great things. On the positive side you are a workaholic, your energies never ebb and you have to keep yourself constantly on the move. It would not suit you to work where you have no freedom of self-expression as you are an extrovert who likes to do well and has no time for the inept or slow-witted.

Many 9s prefer to work for themselves as they do not get on well with employers' rules that do not fit in with their lifestyles. They are adventurous and will be involved in most risk sports or ventures, thriving on excitement. They should be careful that they do not take on more than they can handle as they tend to be Jack of all trades and master of none. They tend to become bored easily and need to be kept on the boil if they are to achieve.

The negative 9 is a bit of an egomaniac; he can be very domineering even to the extent of crushing those who oppose his ideals.

Your numbers vibrate to the planets Mercury, Uranus and Mars.

As a 54/9 you are blessed with the sharp mind and wit of Mercury, the inspirational genius of Uranus and the drive, ambition and energy of Mars to see a job done. People born with this combination of numbers are unpredictable. You are bright, sharp and have an astute mind which can smell a bargain a mile off. You thrive on a sense of adventure that others at times consider madness. You have a high level of physical energy and need to burn it off. You are very restless in younger years with this birth vibration. You exist for the challenge and once conquered you move on to pastures new. There can be periods of mental burn-out but you quickly recover to start anew. In romance you should not make rash promises that you cannot keep, and would find greater security in a later marriage. You have to burn off your dreams before you can commit yourself fully.

As a negative 54/9 you are always starting projects that you do not complete. Your initial enthusiasm is lost when you see what you consider to be a more adventurous enterprise. You can be very impatient and quick tempered. A long term commitment is required in order that you may learn the responsibility of your actions. You should also learn that not everyone has your drive or energy and be more understanding of their inability to keep pace.

Your birth number is 54/9

Name: Date of birth:

Lucky number: Lucky colour:

Partner's birth number:

Positive characteristics:

Negative characteristics:

PATRICE

Your lucky numbers are: 1, 10, 19, 28, 37, 46, 55, 64, 73, 82, 91, 100.
Your lucky colours are: crimson, flame and white.
Your best partners are: other 1s, 4s or 8s.

Your character
As a ruling 1 person you are the father of all numbers. It is the symbol of unity; it stands for ambition, originality, independence and firmness of purpose. Ruling 1s are born leaders. You are very original in thought and action, therefore very creative. You are explorers, pioneers, promoters and organisers. One as a birth number is quite forceful, tending to dominate the environment in which the individual operates.

A negative 1 is arrogant, domineering, egotistical, inconsiderate and selfish, too concerned with his own life to notice the plight of others.

Your numbers vibrate to the planets Mercury and the Sun.

As a 55/1 you are blessed with the sharp intellect and wit of Mercury and the magnetic aura of attraction of the Sun. People born with this combination of numbers have all the ingredients for a successful life. You who were born with this vibration were given a degree of responsibility in order that you may assist the karma of your fellow man. You will be a leader in your own field or community and respected by your peers. The level to which you aspire in your career, home life or community is totally dependent upon your own drive and ambition. If you reach for the stars, then they are yours; if you do not apply yourself, you can blame no-one. Your ability to communicate to the masses would see you well on the road to success in journalism, sales, advertising or the media. In romance, you are flirtatious, though faithful when committed.

As a negative 55/1 you may use your ability to communicate to deceive others or yourself. You will be a materialist who is too short-sighted to see the long-term effects of your actions. You can become ego-centred and selfish. It is no crime in a democratic society to apply yourself and reap the rewards of your labours. It is, however, inhumane to do so at the expense of your fellow man.

Keep a sympathetic ear to the ground and you can't go wrong.

Your birth number is $55/10$

Name: Date of birth:

Lucky number: Lucky colour:

Partner's birth number:

Positive characteristics:

Negative characteristics:

Your birth number is
56/11

Your lucky numbers are: 2, 11, 20, 29, 38, 47, 56, 65, 74, 83, 92.
Your lucky colours are: salmon, grey and navy blue.
Your best partners are: other 2s, 5s or 7s.

Your character
As a ruling 2 you stand for duality, sharing and partnership. You are deeply sensitive and find a great need to share your thoughts and emotions with someone that you feel you can trust with your insecurities. The bonds that you form can become intense, blocking out all else in your life. All 2s are gentle and kind, preferring the peaceful path if at all possible, though they should be careful that others do not misuse this. The greatest fault of 2s is that they can become too sensitive and timid, reacting to extremes of happiness and depression. They should cultivate a bit more of the 'get up and go' of the ruling 1.

Your numbers vibrate to the planets Mercury, Venus and the Moon.

As a 56/2 you are blessed with the sharp mind and wit of Mercury, the artistic beauty and grace of Venus, and the compassion and caring of the Moon. People born with this combination of numbers are very caring and considerate. Your outer shell can be quite chatty and extrovert. This, however, is not the real you. You are, in fact, very sensitive to the thoughts, words and actions of your fellow man. You are very loving and would make an adoring parent. You do enjoy a night out on the town but would much prefer an evening at home with someone you love. If you feel neglected by your chosen mate, your dry wit will soon drop a hint or two.

Although this number may travel, it has strong ties to its own home base and will maintain family ties and commitments. If domestic strife should occur it will do all in its power to make amends. In younger years this number will work harder than most in order to establish a secure family home. These 56/2 people would make great nurses, social workers or probation officers, as they have a sympathetic ear for others' problems.

As a negative 56/2 they may fear that commitment to a partnership that their number desires. They can become overly possessive, constantly testing the loyalty of those around them, driving them away. Subconscious fears, worries and anxieties rise up and threaten to drown them. They can then withdraw from what they think is the Rat Race.

Use your Mercury to express your true feelings and others will assist rather than avoid you.

Your birth number is 56/11

Name: Date of birth:

Lucky number: Lucky colour:

Partner's birth number:

Positive characteristics:

Negative characteristics:

Your birth number is

57/12

Your lucky numbers are: 3, 12, 21, 30, 39, 48, 57, 66, 75, 84, 93.
Your lucky colours are: purple, burgundy and black.
Your best partners are: other 3s, 6s or 9s.

Your character
As a ruling 3 person you are independent both in your mannerisms and speech. You are ultra-adaptable, being able to become the person required of the moment. You show artistic flair and ability and have a vivid imagination. Your versatility is well known among your ever-increasing circle of friends. Ruling 3s make great actors, poets, teachers and salesmen. They have a natural ability that enables them to pick things up very quickly. Their biggest fault is that they can at times spread themselves a bit thin on the ground, having too many balls in the air at one time. Should things go wrong they need no sympathy from others; they generate their own.

Your numbers vibrate to the planets Mercury, Neptune and Jupiter.

As a 57/3 you are blessed with the sharp mind and wit of Mercury, the intuition and insight of Neptune and the philosophy and adventure of Jupiter. People born with this combination of numbers are pleasant and jovial. Variety is the spice of life to these people. They have the ability to put ideas into practical reality. They can be the life and soul of the party or social gathering and may be known as practical jokers. In romance they are chatty and can flit from partner to partner until they find their fun-loving opposite, then they are committed and will remain faithful unless they consider their mate is becoming boring. People born with this combination of numbers appear to have more than their fair share of luck; although they may worry about what may happen, they always appear to land on their feet. The 57/3s make great entertainers.

As a negative 57/3 you may be the life and soul of the party, but you make promises that you fail to keep. You zealously commit yourself to many projects but can become easily bored and fail to complete them. Your sharp wit and dry humour can turn to sarcasm. Though still fairly popular, you will become known as unreliable. Start one project at a time and see it through to its end and you will be on the road to the success you desire.

Your birth number is 57/12

Name: Date of birth:

Lucky number: Lucky colour:

Partner's birth number:

Positive characteristics:

Negative characteristics:

Your birth number is
58/13

Your lucky numbers are: 4, 13, 22, 31, 40, 49, 58, 67, 76, 85, 94.
Your lucky colours are: blue, green and indigo.
Your best partners are: other 4s, 1s or 8s.

Your character

As a positive ruling 4 you are a builder, both on the material and the intellectual planes, always busy mentally and physically. A 4 makes a splendid bookmaker or mechanic; he is mathematical, methodical and a master of detail and routine. He is a splendid builder of systems for greater economy. His ambitions are of a personal nature for his own self-development. All 4s need a firm platform from which to operate. Once this is achieved they find themselves free from the worries and fears that held them back from their ideals and dreams in the first place. Go on, commit yourself.

As a negative 4 you are despondent, buried beneath adverse circumstances, financial limitations and hard work, a plodder without any desire for intellectual development.

Your numbers vibrate to the planets Mercury, Saturn and Uranus.

You are blessed with the sharp mind and wit of Mercury, the maturity and practicality of Saturn and the inspirational genius of Uranus. People born with this combination of birth numbers are very creative and inventive. In romance they mature young. They have responsibilities thrust upon them in younger years. They are the builders, politicians, civil servants and community workers of our society.

You are a builder on the material plane in your younger years. However, as you grow older, the desire to do and see all the things that you feel you missed in your youth will be achieved. For you, life begins at forty. Though you may not receive public recognition for your contribution to a smooth running democracy, it is a certainty that without your behind-the-scenes endeavours society as we know it would come to a halt.

As a negative 58/4 your insecurities and anxieties can cause you to rebel against that which you fear in society. If taken too far there can be a danger of isolation. You may become distrustful and self-indulgent. Instead of working for society and building for the benefit of all, your insecurity turns you into a materially self-orientated person. Remember that in a democracy rules are made for the benefit of the majority not minority.

Your birth number is $^{58}/_{13}$

Name: Date of birth:

Lucky number: Lucky colour:

Partner's birth number:

Positive characteristics:

Negative characteristics:

Your lucky numbers are: 5, 14, 23, 32, 41, 50, 59, 68, 77, 86, 95.
Your lucky colours are: scarlet, orange and wine.
Your best partners are: other 5s, 2s or 7s.

Your character
As a ruling 5 person you are a wanderer. Mental activity is strong with these people; they just don't seem able to find the neutral gear as far as mental activity is concerned, always full of bright ideas and projects. The number is sometimes called the freedom seeker, as the ruling 5 is always on the go. He loves to travel and hates restrictions of any kind. Fives are best employed in a job that has few restrictions as they hate regulations. Quick-witted and with few inhibitions, these people are usually found in the positions of stress that others find difficult to control.

The negative 5, on the other hand, is the chatterbox who rants on endlessly and says very little, too pre-occupied with his own ego and self-praise to notice that he is boring the pants off his friends. Ulcers or stress-orientated illnesses prevail and there can be a tendency to mental burn-outs which leave him dazed and disorientated.

Your numbers vibrate to the planets Mercury and Mars.

As a 59/5 you are blessed with the sharp mind, intellect and wit of Mercury and the energy, drive and ambition of Mars. People born with this combination of numbers excel in situations that are stressful. You were born with an exceptionally high level of mental activity. The combination of mentality and energy can give creative genius; on the other hand, if allowed to run out of control, anxiety and depression take over. Those of you born with this birth number definitely need some form of physical activity to help you to burn off the excess energy. This number is outwardly quite extrovert, although there are undertones of nervous tension. Careers best suited to these people are the ones with few regulations and as much travel and variety as possible. They could make great sailors, as in romance they may have a girl in every port. They thrive upon challenge. However, all is not forsaken. Once the wanderlust of adolescence has run its course they could be an asset to any business, corporation or concern. Their great ambition to succeed sees they get the top jobs with maturity.

As a negative 59/5 you are Jack of all trades yet master of none. Your ability to assimilate and learn things quickly can lead you to become impatient and bad-tempered with us less gifted mortals.

If you wish stability in career or romance, then you must endeavour to find an everlasting challenge as, once you have overcome a challenge, you become bored easily and quickly move on to pastures new.

Your birth number is $59/14$

Name: Date of birth:

Lucky number: Lucky colour:

Partner's birth number:

Positive characteristics:

Negative characteristics:

Your lucky numbers are: 6, 15, 24, 33, 42, 51, 60, 69, 78, 87, 96.
Your lucky colours are: bitter chocolate, green and deep sea blue.
Your best partners are: other 6s, 9s and 3s.

Your character
As a ruling 6 person you are kind and gentle-hearted, generous and peaceful, striving constantly to put right other people's wrongs. You are known for your adoration of children and the beautiful, artistic things of life with which you try to surround yourself. You would make an excellent nurse or social worker and can see both sides of most coins. You do like an active social life though you need the knowledge that you have a safe, secure home to retreat to. You may be very house-proud as you like your surroundings to look pleasing and be admired by visitors.

You can, on the negative side, be very vain, always admiring your own accomplishments and expecting others to do the same. Your ardent love for the home and family can cause you to find it difficult to break away on your own.

Your number vibrates to the planet Venus.

As a 60/6 you are blessed with the beauty, poise, grace and artistic ability of Venus raised to the power of 10. People born with this birth number are extremely sensitive, artistic and reactive to their surroundings. This birth number symbolises the planet Venus in its purest sense. If there was a queue for good looks, artistic ability and sensitivity, you were given a place near the front at the time of your birth. This birth is the eternal, all-caring mother of society. Women with this birth number make excellent mothers of large families. They make great painters, sculptors, fashion designers, in fact, anything requiring creativity. They are very faithful and possessive lovers and although they require a great deal of admiration for their personal appearance or a job well done, they do not accept criticism easily. A 60/6 has the world at his feet.

As a negative 60/6 you allow vanity, ego and your own high opinion of yourself to blot out all else, to your own detriment. The imagination becomes overwrought and the slightest flaw in your appearance becomes a scar.

You were given your artistic ability and appreciation of the finer things of life in order that could share it with your fellow man. Do not allow your vanity to destroy this gift of gifts.

Your birth number is ⁶⁰/₆

Name: Date of birth:

Lucky number: Lucky colour:

Partner's birth number:

Positive characteristics:

Negative characteristics:

Your birth number is
61/7

Your lucky numbers are: 7, 16, 25, 34, 43, 52, 61, 70, 79, 88, 97.
Your lucky colours are: sky blue, silver and sea green.
Your best partners are: other 7s, 5s or 2s.

Your character
As a ruling 7 person you are highly intuitive, constantly gathering information on the mysteries of life but seldom talking about them. A deep thinker but not a great doer, you are seldom understood by others and tend to withdraw. Your inability to express the real you can often lead you into a life of semi-seclusion, preferring to keep your own counsel because others just don't seem to understand what you are trying to say.

The negative 7 lives in a world all of his own, preferring to romanticise and dream rather than face up to the realities of life. He should learn to understand that not all things can be as in our dreams, a perfect match.

Your numbers vibrate to the planets Venus, Sun and Neptune.

As a 61/7 you are blessed with the poise, beauty and grace of Venus, the magnetic aura and attraction of the Sun and the intuitive insight of Neptune. People born with this birth vibration are the spiritual backbone of society. The artistic and sensitive vibrations of life are raised to a more spiritual level with this birth vibration. Many people born under its influence may show marked psychic or mediumistic ability.

Few people in the material world in which we live can cope or exist on such a spiritual number. It therefore may revert to its more material vibration of insecurity, anxiety and nervousness. However, it can possess artistic genius. In romance people with this birth number would require a very understanding mate who is able to keep pace with this artistic temperament. A career in the arts or related fields would suit this birth vibration.

As a negative 61/7 there can be a tendency to neurotic disorders, anxieties and a dread of the unknown. The creativity instead of finding its normal expression turns inwardly, which can cause the individual to live in a fantasy. Such creative genius can border on insanity, and people with this birth vibration tend to lack emotional balance, being either ecstatically happy or totally depressed. They must learn to achieve a balance between the two.

Your birth number is 61/7

Name: Date of birth:

Lucky number: Lucky colour:

Partner's birth number:

Positive characteristics:

Negative characteristics:

Your birth number is
62/8

Your lucky numbers are: 8, 17, 26, 35, 44, 53, 62, 71, 80, 89, 98.
Your lucky colours are: black and all dark shades, such as burgundy.
Your best partners are: other 8s, 4s or 1s.

Your character

As a ruling 8 person you are a materialist. People born under this vibration have great business heads and management ability. They prefer things they can measure or see in a real way and scoff at the dreamers. They make great bankers, lawyers, stock brokers, etc. They love a challenge and their ability to wait for the right moment usually sees them in the top jobs and positions of their chosen careers. They don't like losers.

Many politicians vibrate to an 8 as they achieve success in their business and seek out new challenges to tax their managerial ability.

The negative 8, on the other hand, is out of touch with reality, always wanting to start at the top of his chosen field without realising he may have the ability but not the experience.

Your numbers vibrate to the planets Venus, Moon and Saturn.

As a 62/8 you are blessed with the artistic abilities of Venus, coupled with the compassion and caring of the Moon and the practical outlets of Saturn. You are very sympathetic to a ready cause but will have no sympathy for a hypochondriac. Although you sometimes wish your work-load would be lightened, you always end up doing the job yourself as then you know it is well done. You can at times have a tendency to put things off that you feel are not so important. This, however, can catch up with you and cause inconvenience.

In romance you are very loyal, though the partnership is much more settled in the second half of life. You fear stress and yet it is under stress that your intuition comes to your aid and saves the day. Children are rarely plentiful but always guarded and protected. Wealth comes to a 62/8 through long-term projects and hard work. A career in social work or the , civil service would suit the 62/8 but there can also be exceptional artistic or design ability. More would depend on environmental circumstances. You are usually a great lover of pets.

As a negative 62/8 your life will stem around trying to find a life partner of your dreams, who may not exist. Your desire for reassurance can cause you to help those who do not want it; though your intentions may have been honourable, you can be considered nosy by others. You need to concentrate more upon your excessive imagination. If you always wish for the best, you are often disappointed, therefore take things for what they are and endeavour to shape them into your dreams. Your discontentment will then disappear. All 8s must learn by their own trial and error.

Your birth number is 62/8

Name: Date of birth:

Lucky number: Lucky colour:

Partner's birth number:

Positive characteristics:

Negative characteristics:

Your birth number is
63/9

Your lucky numbers are: 9, 18, 27, 36, 45, 54, 63, 72, 81, 90, 99.
Your lucky colours are: scarlet, red and orange.
Your best partners are: other 9s, 3s or 6s.

Your character
As a ruling 9 person you are supercharged full of energy, vitality and the will to achieve great things. On the positive side you are a workaholic, your energies never ebb and you have to keep yourself constantly on the move. It would not suit you to work where you have no freedom of self expression as you are an extrovert who likes to do well and has no time for the inept or slow-witted.

Many 9s prefer to work for themselves as they do not get on well with employers' rules that do not fit in well with their lifestyles. They are adventurous and will be involved with most risk sports or ventures, thriving on excitement. They should be careful that they do not take on more than they can handle as they tend to be Jack of all trades and master of none. They tend to become bored easily so need to be kept on the boil if they are to achieve.

The negative 9 is a bit of an egomaniac who can be very domineering even to the extent of crushing those who oppose his ideals.

Your numbers vibrate to the planets Venus, Jupiter and Mars.

As a 63/9 you are blessed with the artistic compassion of Venus, the philosophical insight of Jupiter and the energy and aggression of Mars. People born with this combination of numbers are usually socially much sought after, popular, active in sports or community activities. Twenty-four hours a day sometimes seems too short for people with this vibration.

Rash and impetuous as you are at times, things always seem to work out for the best in the end, no matter how severe you thought it would be. Variety is the spice of life to you and fighting the repetition of a boring job or routine is your biggest obstacle in life. In romance, you require a mate who stands up to you and is your equal. While you like partners to show their feelings and loyalties, you also require a mate who is not possessive and allows you freedom of self-expression. Children, usually two or three, are well cared for, though expected to be strong and independent as they grow up. Work in any field of sales is good.

Monetary wealth comes and goes for these 63/9 people as they tend to spend what they earn, be it large or small.

As a negative 63/9 your desire for freedom, fun and pleasure can lead to a lonely inner life, and the stable, long-term relationship you are looking for may never materialise.

The glitter and gleam of your social life can cause ulcers or stress-orientated illnesses as you try to keep up your reputation as a 'who dares, wins' type. Endeavour to have a secure rest place to return to, away from the public eye, in order that you may recuperate for your next adventure.

Your birth number is $^{63}/_{9}$

Name: Date of birth:

Lucky number: Lucky colour:

Partner's birth number:

Positive characteristics:

Negative characteristics:

Your birth number is
64/1

Your lucky numbers are: 1, 10, 19, 28, 37, 46, 55, 64, 73, 82, 91, 100.
Your lucky colours are: crimson, flame and white.
Your best partners are: other 1s, 4s or 8s.

Your character
As a ruling 1 person you are the father of all numbers. It is the
symbol of unity; it stands for ambition, originality, independence
and firmness of purpose. Ruling 1s are born leaders. You are very
original in thought and action, therefore very creative. You are
explorers, pioneers, promoters, organisers. One as a birth number
is quite forceful, tending to dominate the environment in which
the individual operates.

A negative 1 is arrogant, domineering, egotistical, inconsiderate
and selfish, too concerned with his own life to notice the plight of
others.

Your numbers vibrate to the planets Venus, Uranus and Sun.

As a 64/1 you are blessed with the artistic expression of Venus
coupled with the reactive genius of Uranus, working through the
independence of the Sun. This combination of numbers can make
you a bit of a loner. It is a higher vibration of the leader of the new
Aquarian age and your ideals or ambitions will not initially conform with the majority of the society of your time. It is the number
of the change-bringer and such a task may be a lonely path if you
should choose to follow it.

On a more mundane level there is artistic ability, though more
on the logical organising level, and it is in your ability to organise

others that you will find the success and material security that you seek. In romance you are very loyal, though it may take you a little longer to commit yourself to your chosen mate.

On the negative side, 64/1 people will desire positions of power or authority that they may have the capabilities for but perhaps not the experience. They will rebel against the current society, feeling that it is against them and the changes they wish to make for the good of all, or so they think. They need to learn to take one step at a time up the ladder as, if they run up, they may slip on a rung and fall with a loud bang.

Managerial or supervisory work should come to these people if they learn to take orders as well as sometimes give them.

Your birth number is 64/1

Name: Date of birth:

Lucky number: Lucky colour:

Partner's birth number:

Positive characteristics:

Negative characteristics:

Your birth number is
65/2

Your lucky numbers are: 2, 11, 20, 29, 38, 47, 56, 65, 74, 83, 92.
Your lucky colours are: salmon, grey and navy blue.
Your best partners are: other 2s, 5s or 7s.

Your character

As a ruling 2 you stand for duality, sharing and partnership. You are deeply sensitive and feel a great need to share your thoughts and emotions with someone that you feel you can trust with your insecurities. The bonds that you form can become intense, blocking out all else in your life. All 2s are gentle and kind, preferring the peaceful path if at all possible, though they should be careful that others do not misuse this.

The greatest fault of 2s is that they can become too sensitive and timid, reacting to extremes of happiness and depression. You should cultivate a bit more of the 'get up and go' of the ruling 1.

Your numbers vibrate to the planets Venus, Mercury and Moon.

As a 65/2 you are blessed with the artistic beauty and grace of Venus coupled with the sharp mind and quick wit of Mercury working through the compassion of the Moon.

People born with these vibrations were born of a generation that was to undergo great changes in society and the social order. They were born with an understanding and intuition of these changes in order that they might make their fellow man understand. On a more mundane level, they are deeply sensitive people, initially shy and thoughtful, seeking emotional security and equilibrium in themselves. Once this is obtained they are a bottomless well of sympathy, understanding and compassion for friends, families or associates that have need of a shoulder to cry on.

In romance they are very loyal partners, ultra-supportive of their mates' desires or needs and very loving parents. This can materialise in a larger way through charities or famine relief, wherein they become parents for all the needy in the world.

The negative 65/2 fails to understand or control his emotional feelings, sense of insecurity and desire to test the loyalty or motives of those around him, which leaves him dissatisfied with his lot. He fears the changes that take place in society and misinterprets the meaning of those changes. There can be a danger of isolation and a tendency to stress-orientated illnesses. He must learn to let go of old, outdated concepts and become a part of what is transpiring around him, in order that he may find the stability and security he needs. If he bottles up his emotions for too long the outpouring of emotions, when it comes, will be too much for his partner to handle.

Learn to trust others more and share your inner feelings with your mate rather than your imaginations.

Your birth number is 65/2

Name: Date of birth:

Lucky number: Lucky colour:

Partner's birth number:

Positive characteristics:

Negative characteristics:

117

Your birth number is
66/3

Your lucky numbers are: 3, 12, 21, 30, 39, 48, 57, 66, 75, 84, 93.
Your lucky colours are: purple, burgundy and black.
Your best partners are: other 3s, 6s and 9s.

Your character
As a ruling 3 person you are independent both in your mannerisms and speech. You are ultra-adaptable, being able to become
the person required of the moment. You show artistic flair and
ability and a vivid imagination. Your versatility is well known
among your ever-increasing circle of friends. Ruling 3s make great
actors, poets, teachers and salesmen. They have a natural ability
that enables them to pick things up very quickly. Their biggest
fault is that they can at times spread themselves a bit too thin on
the ground, having too many balls in the air at one time. Should
things go wrong, they need no sympathy from others; they
generate their own.

Your numbers vibrate to the planets Venus and Jupiter.

As a 66/3 you are blessed with the artistic, creative and loving
nature of Venus working through the philosophic, beneficial
nature of Jupiter. This birth number has only just occurred for the
fifth time this century, i.e. 31 + 12 + 1 + 9 + 8 + 5. The last
occurrence was 31 + 12 + 1976 when the technological revolution
began for real – progress in science, medicine and cultural differ-
ences through world travel. It would appear from these indica-
tions that a generation of children have been born who will grow
up to become the inventors and originators of the changes that we

shall have around us with the coming of the Aquarian age and the year 2000. Those individuals born in the latter days of the latter months of 1949, 1958, 1967, 1976, 1985 and those yet to be born in the 1990s will have been active in the changes in the thoughts and actions of the general masses either for good or bad.

Your birth number is $^{66}/_3$

Name: Date of birth:

Lucky number: Lucky colour:

Partner's birth number:

Positive characteristics:

Negative characteristics:

Your birth number is
67/4

Your lucky numbers are: 4, 13, 22, 31, 40, 49, 58, 67, 76, 85, 94.
Your lucky colours are: blue, green and indigo.
Your best partners are: other 4s, 1s or 8s.

Your character
As a positive ruling 4 you are a builder, both on the material and the intellectual planes, always busy mentally and physically. A 4 makes a splendid bookmaker or mechanic; he is mathematical, methodical, a master of routine and detail. He is a splendid builder of systems for greater economy. His ambitions are of a personal nature for his own self-development. All 4s need a firm platform from which to operate. Once this is achieved they find themselves free from the worries and fears that held them back from their ideals and dreams in the first place. Go on, commit yourself.

As a negative 4 you are despondent, buried beneath adverse circumstances, financial limitations and hard work, a plodder without any desire for intellectual development.

Your numbers vibrate to the planets Venus, Neptune and Uranus.

As a 67/4 you are born with the artistic imagination of Uranus and Neptune, coupled with the insight and higher mind of Uranus. The first time this vibration appeared this century was 31.12.59, so it must be seen as those effects upon society in the Sixties and Seventies as this generation of people grew up. The political, social and environmental changes and the nuclear era of

120

power, and the conflicts that come with it, seem to vibrate to this combination of numbers. People concerned with the earth, ecology and nature's survival seem to be a part of this vibration. So too is personal freedom to express the qualities of the individual rather than the mass.

The number seems also to have some effect on religious movements of a more unorthodox nature. Be this through feminism or not, I feel the strength of women and the suffering of mankind to be a part of this number's effect on society as a whole.

If you were born with this vibration you have some task to perform to prepare later generations for the future of man. This number also occurred at the end of the Victorian era last century – 31.12.1869.

Your birth number is $^{67}/_4$

Name: Date of birth:

Lucky number: Lucky colour:

Partner's birth number:

Positive characteristics:

Negative characteristics:

Your lucky numbers are: 5, 14, 23, 32, 41, 50, 59, 68, 77, 86, 95.
Your lucky colours are: scarlet, orange and wine.
Your best partners are: other 5s, 2s or 7s.

Your character
As a ruling 5 person you are a wanderer. Mental activity is strong with these people; they just don't seem to be able to find the neutral gear as far as mental activity is concerned, always full of bright ideas and projects. The number is sometimes called the freedom seeker, as the ruling 5 is always on the go, loves to travel and hates restrictions of any kind. Fives are best employed in a job that has few restrictions as they hate regulations. Quick-witted and with few inhibitions, these people are usually found in the positions of stress that others find difficult to control.

The negative 5, on the other hand, is the chatterbox who rants on endlessly and says very little, too preoccupied with his own ego and self-praise to notice that he is boring the pants off his friends. Ulcers or stress-orientated illnesses prevail and there can be a tendency to mental burn-outs which leave him dazed and disorientated.

Your numbers vibrate to the planets Venus, Saturn and Mercury.

As a 68/5 you are the communicators of the society of the 1980s. This vibration first occurred this century on 31.12.1969. Those born under its influence are the people who rule the higher level upon which we all communicate today: computer technology, man's desire to travel to the stars, laser and light technology. People with this vibration will be the ones who turn ideas into concrete realities: the changes in communication in our homes through the media and TV, the growing number of satellites, and so on. It is the demands made upon or created by this vibration that have caused these changes. These people are the freedom seekers, fighters, that we see in society today, extreme in their belief in a new era or trying to hold onto an old outdated concept, be they positive or negative.

People born under this combination may be torn between the social conditioning of the old society that appears safe and secure and the creation of a new age that appears in their visions. They must learn to reach for and accept the changes that occur around them as they are the communicators of the future of man.

Your birth number is $^{68}/_5$

Name: Date of birth:

Lucky number: Lucky colour:

Partner's birth number:

Positive characteristics:

Negative characteristics:

Your birth number is
69/6

Your lucky numbers are: 6, 15, 24, 33, 42, 51, 60, 69, 78, 87, 96.
Your lucky colours are: bitter chocolate, green and deep sea blue.
Your best partners are: other 6s, 9s and 3s.

Your character
As a ruling 6 person you are kind and gentle-hearted, generous and peaceful, striving constantly to put right other people's wrongs. You are known for your adoration of children and the beautiful, artistic things of life with which you try to surround yourself. You would make an excellent nurse or social worker and can see both sides of most coins. You do like an active social life though you need the knowledge that you have a safe, secure home to retreat to. You may be very house-proud as you like your surroundings to look pleasing and be admired by visitors.

You can, on the negative side, be very vain, always admiring your own accomplishments and expecting others to do the same. Your ardent love for the home and family cause you to find it difficult to break away on your own.

Your numbers vibrate to the planets Venus and Mars.

As a 69/6 has so far only occurred once this century and the next occurrence is not until 1988, we can only judge them according to changes in the previous century and the effects that occurred around 20 years after its last occurrence in 1889.

It appears to have been at a time when the masses rose up against the society of old, when unemployment was high and war was just over the horizon. Mars on the one hand rules war and aggression while Venus on the other rules peace and beauty, so I can only surmise that people born under this vibration are the ones who will bring order out of chaos, and if they must fight for those beliefs, then so be it. If you are born with this combination of numbers, you must force yourself to stand up for your beliefs. Strive for your ambitions and beliefs for, although you may feel oppressed or subjugated, if you persevere and remain true to your beliefs you cannot fail to achieve that which you desire in the end, though a touch of sadness will always be your lot as you may be apt to over-reach or expect too much too soon at times.

Your birth number is 6%

Name: Date of birth:

Lucky number: Lucky colour:

Partner's birth number:

Positive characteristics:

Negative characteristics:

Your birth number is
70/7

Your lucky numbers are: 7, 16, 25, 34, 43, 52, 61, 70, 79, 88, 97.
Your lucky colours are: sky blue, silver and sea green.
Your best partners are: other 7s, 5s or 2s.

Your character
As a ruling 7 person you are highly intuitive, constantly gathering information on the mysteries of life, but seldom talking about them. A deep thinker but not a great doer, you are seldom understood by others and tend to withdraw. Your inability to express the real you can often lead you into a life of semi-seclusion, preferring to keep your own counsel because others just don't seem to understand what you are trying to say.

The negative 7 lives in a world all of his own, preferring to romanticise and dream rather than face up to the realities of life. He should learn to understand that not all things can be as in our dreams, a perfect match.

Your numbers vibrate to Neptune.

As a 70/7 you have yet to be born this century. This combination of numbers last appeared in and on only one date, 31.12.1899, and will not occur again until 31.12.1989. When it occurs this century Neptune will be transiting Capricorn and its effects can then be judged. However, people born with a 7 raised to a power of 10 must be those who will bring the peace and harmony predicted through the oracles of the ages.

The 1920s was a time of fun, gaiety and expansion before the decline in world economics of the 1930s. So again we can only assume that those born under this number will be the bringers of fun, art and laughter, helping us to forget for a time at least the problems that surround us in the world in the first decade of the next century. The force of Neptune is deceptive; it works upon the subconscious rather than the conscious. Therefore people born under this number will be behind the scenes manipulating the greater masses, taking our minds off the problems we face, striving to overcome the realities of tomorrow.

This vibration requires more research to be fully understood.

Your birth number is 70/7

Name: Date of birth:

Lucky number: Lucky colour:

Partner's birth number:

Positive characteristics:

Negative characteristics:

Your Birth Number Interpretation

If you require a full interpretation of your birth and name numbers on a 60-minute cassette, send full details of your name, address and date of birth with a cheque for £15.00 to

W. Foulsham & Co. Ltd.
Birth Number Interpretation
Yeovil Road
Slough
Berkshire
SL1 4JH

Allow 29 days for delivery.